P9-BAW-070

Please remember that this is a library book,
and that it belongs only temporarily to each
person who uses it. Be considerate. Do
not write in this, or any, library book.

Oral History
in Social Work

SAGE HUMAN SERVICES GUIDES

A series of books edited by ARMAND LAUFFER and CHARLES D. GARVIN. Published in cooperation with the University of Michigan School of Social Work and other organizations.

ΑΔΥ-6692
VC Grad

Oral History in Social Work

Research, Assessment, and Intervention

Ruth R. Martin

SHSG SAGE HUMAN SERVICES GUIDE 69

*Published in cooperation with the University
of Michigan School of Social Work*

SAGE Publications
International Educational and Professional Publisher
Thousand Oaks   London   New Delhi

Copyright © 1995 by Sage Publications, Inc.

All rights reserved. No part of this book may be reproduced or utilized in any form or by any means, electronic or mechanical, including photocopying, recording, or by any information storage and retrieval system, without permission in writing from the publisher.

For information address:

 SAGE Publications, Inc.
2455 Teller Road
Thousand Oaks, California 91320
E-mail: order@sagepub.com

SAGE Publications Ltd.
6 Bonhill Street
London EC2A 4PU
United Kingdom

SAGE Publications India Pvt. Ltd.
M-32 Market
Greater Kailash I
New Delhi 110 048 India

Printed in the United States of America

Library of Congress Cataloging-in-Publication Data

Martin, Ruth R.
Oral history in social work: Research, assessment, and
intervention / Ruth R. Martin.
        p.   cm.   —(Sage human services guides; vol. 69)
    Includes bibliographical references and index.
    ISBN 0-8039-4382-2 (cloth: alk. paper).   —   ISBN 0-8039-4383-0 (pbk.:
alk. paper)
    1. Social service—Methodology. 2. Human services—Methodology.
3. Oral history—Methodology. I. Title. II. Series: Sage human services
guides; v. 69.
HV41.M285   1995
361.3'2—dc20   95-17009

This book is printed on acid-free paper.

95   96   97   98   99   10   9   8   7   6   5   4   3   2   1

Sage Production Editor: Gillian Dickens

ACCORDING to an old African proverb, "it takes a whole village to raise a child." This book is dedicated to my village (community), to my people, yes, to you—the many people whose sacrifices, struggles, survivals, teachings, strengths, courage, love, and prayers pushed me onward.

To my parents, Joe Robinson and Beatrice Hodges Robinson, who taught me how to persevere to achieve. I know that your spirits watch over me always.

To my husband, Rutrell, whose love and support have sustained me. You gave me space to grow and the length of time necessary—even though it took longer than either of us expected.

To our children—Vivian, Rutrell, Maxine, Sonya, Anthony, and Valerie—my life's true blessings. Each has been a catalyst as motivators, research assistants, copy editors, typists, and transcribers. You never doubted I could complete this book nor allowed me to rest until I did.

To my siblings, aunts, nieces, and cousins: I am lucky that you were in my village.

CONTENTS

PREFACE

More than 40 years ago, as I worked toward my bachelor's degree in secondary education, my methods teacher, Vernon McDaniel, admonished the class, "Anybody can be a good teacher." He challenged, "What you want to be is a great teacher. In order to do so, you must add to the profession." This book, then, is my attempt to respond, if only in part, to Professor McDaniel's challenge.

The book offers oral history research as a multifaceted approach to social work practice and other human service programs. The major focus of the book is to provide information to human service professionals and others about the importance of oral history as a useful research, assessment, and intervention tool and as a vehicle for integrating minority group content in social work education and practice. The book is appropriate for all levels of social work education (human services, bachelor's, master's, and doctorate). It can also be useful for research in substantive areas such as Black experiences, elderly, women, and health and in teaching about human diversity and human oppression. It is suitable for educational development purposes and with client populations for empowerment. In addition, it can help in researching one's own family tree and heritage.

Through the interview process, practitioners can strengthen the knowledge base of the profession as they learn to communicate across social, racial, class, and sexual barriers and find some entry into the lives of those who have been left out or oppressed by the system. The implications for the profession are many, including contribution to professional knowledge, values communication, development of assessment skills, and intervention and teaching methodology.

The purpose of the book is to demonstrate the ways in which the form of qualitative research called oral history and the nature of social work practice complement each other. I give examples of this throughout the book. In Chapter 3, I specifically make a bridge from social work practice knowledge and the human services in general to oral history research skills. I hope this book serves as a catalyst, challenging researchers, practitioners, educators, and other adult learners to build on the knowledge and applications suggested in these pages.

ACKNOWLEDGMENTS

One does not complete work on a book without building on the knowledge and thoughtful criticism of those in the profession who have paved the way. In that, I thank those whose works have helped me develop and grow. I acknowledge the many people who in various ways contributed to the completion of this book. I am especially grateful to the many people who shared their stories, without whom this work could not have begun.

I thank Professor Judith A. B. Lee—my colleague, friend, and cheerleader—who has always been there for me and supportive of my work. Her editorial assistance was critical to completion of this work. I also thank my colleague Professor Martin Bloom, whose reading of the work helped me to more critically differentiate between research and practice. My thanks go also to Bruce Stave, professor of history and director of the Center for Oral History at the University of Connecticut, who willingly took time from his busy schedule to read and discuss the oral history technique.

My deep gratitude goes to Virginia Starkie and Pamela Harrison for their patience and secretarial skills during the past 3½ years. I thank my daughter Sonya for her marathon word processing and my daughter Maxine for her transcribing and copy editing. My daughter Vivian—my inspirational, self-appointed researcher—kept me on track when I was sure I could not think another thought. Her "have a cup of tea" or "get a good night's sleep and start again" was constant. I also thank Nancy Humphreys, who supported my efforts by giving her time as she read the manuscript.

My appreciation goes to both my academic institutions, which supported my efforts: The University of South Florida for giving me the first grant to begin the oral history process and the support services of the secretaries and graduate assistants; and my current University of Connecticut, whose grants, travel, and other support services have been invaluable in my continued research and teaching efforts.

To my colleagues, students, and friends I have not named who listened and encouraged me through the years as I processed every new meaning, thank you. I promise to give your ears a rest. And to Armand Lauffer and Sage Publications, thank you for your help and support.

INTRODUCTION

My first remembered experience with the power, magic, excitement, and mystique of storytelling occurred when I was 11. For months, family, friends, relatives, and neighbors had gathered at my home to observe the old tradition of visiting the very sick and "sitting up" most of the night. Actually, some people never seemed to go home.

On this particular night, I was more upset than usual. My younger brother and I had gone to my Aunt Anna's house to bring her to our house. All along the way, she left word for my half brother to "come tonight" if he wanted to see his father alive. "He is not expected to live through the night." I knew that my father was seriously ill, but this was the first time that I was forced to face the reality of his impending death.

That night, I sat huddled in a corner, rooted to the spot, afraid to move a muscle, as my uncle, Cleave Smith, joined by other elderly people, told old stories about every subject imaginable, including long-ago deaths. Many of the topics included so-called conversations the dying had held with their families about whether they had led a good life and were spiritually ready to meet their Maker. He told the stories of Jesus coming in the clouds, the chariot wheels rolling, the feeling of death as it entered the room (now I'm cringing). He quoted statements of one dying person saying, "I cannot see you, or hear you because I am looking into another world, but I want you to meet me in heaven." He did not end there but described what he called "the death rattle." Finally, he summarized these persons' lives as lived and determined whether they had made it into "heaven" or . . .

That night, I learned the meaning the elderly placed on death and on living right. But most of all, I was fascinated at the power Uncle Cleave had to tell a story, to hold the audience, and to bring the past to life. During the course of my life, years after that long night of waiting for the Angel of Death to enter my father's room, I have come to realize the meaning of the story. Yet not until I conducted my first oral history interview did I realize the richness of what my generation learned from our ancestors— not only about death but about living and enjoyment, adaptations and strengths, and the meaning of "giving your word." Giving your word and keeping it defines who you are as a person.

IT'S BEEN A LONG TIME COMING

I began gathering material for this book more than 12 years ago. It grew out of graduate students' curiosity and concern about how to practice with African Americans who reside in the Gulf Coast area of Florida. At the time, Blacks represented more than 13% of the rapidly growing population of approximately 647,000. My need to know was generated as a result of my search for material I could use in teaching a graduate social work class about practice with minority families. The course developed as experiential learning. How, I wondered, could I teach students to practice with populations they knew so little about?

As a newcomer to the community, I was short on local information and understanding. By going to "the people," I reasoned we could learn from the same populations students might soon be serving. I was looking for a new, more direct and engaging way of learning. I had a strong conviction that social workers should take into account the way in which people perceive themselves, their histories and their experiences, and the meanings they attach to their perspectives. This is especially true for those whose experiences have been shaped by the consequences of discrimination. As the mother in Hansberry's *A Raisin in the Sun* (1958) said, "When you judge him, judge him right" (p. 125). To be able to do this, I concluded that social workers must have direct experience with people who have felt the effect of discrimination. I have always been a proponent of experiential learning and thought that by moving the class into a community environment, students would have the opportunity, perhaps for the first time, to experience feelings of being the minority in a minority community set within the wider majority culture.

The focus was on the Black and Latin American communities. The program design was appropriate for teaching about any ethnic group. Some students revealed a complete lack of knowledge about the African American[1] experience. This was true of some African American students as well as of students from the majority culture. In fact, some Blacks seemed to perceive their own race through the lenses of Whites and were not as responsive to the other Blacks. Black clients sometimes sensed this. Some also felt that they were not getting the best social worker if he or she was Black. If this was the case, White and African American students could benefit from a new way of knowing about the Black experience. Both groups could develop the understanding and sensitivity necessary for social work practice. African American students could strengthen their sense of identity and racial pride.

The Tampa area is rich with different cultures. The ethnic makeup of the community includes Seminole Indians, who played an important part in Tampa's heritage; Blacks, who have been a part of Tampa's history from its early beginning; and the Latin American community, which includes Puerto Ricans, the before- and after-Castro Cubans, and the Old World Spanish who have developed their own enclaves. In the Tampa area also are Vietnamese, Haitians, Italians, and Jewish people.

Although I recognized the need for students to integrate knowledge of all of these cultures, it seemed realistic to narrow the focus to those populations that they were most likely to encounter in practice. The graduate social work program at the University of South Florida is a clinical program that is based on a biopsychosocial model. It was necessary, therefore, to design a structure of teaching the African American and Latin American experience that would relate to the clinical model and that would be experiential.

Early in the program, I met with community leaders and service providers. We discussed the possibility of including a group of clients or a client group. To do this, we moved the class into the communities and used the citizens from the communities to address the class in their community setting. The citizens from the Black community included one retired principal, two practicing attorneys, the president of the only African American-controlled bank, members of the educational board, the director of the Urban League, parents, and a panel of four African American clinical social workers. There were also comparable groups from the Latino communities, including a hospital administrator and the state attorney general. The Urban League was used as a classroom in the African American community. The Centro Asturiano Hospital, founded in 1902, was used as the classroom in the Latino community.

The students and I were mesmerized by the sheer knowledge of all the history we heard and all that we saw of human behavior and functioning as we toured the Spanish newspaper office; the African American newspaper office; the Spanish, Cuban, and Italian clubs; cigar factories; and the poor neighborhoods with projects. The plan also included exposing students to lunch in the communities' restaurants. It was not so much the events of this endeavor that excited these future practitioners but the meanings these participants gave to these events. I asked for and received names of people who could contribute to community education centered on a list of selected issues.

The students also read and reported on an autobiography from an assigned literary reference list and other historical novels. For the first time, some members of the class read such books as Angelou's *I Know Why the Caged Bird Sings* (1970), Wright's *Black Boy* (1945), Hansberry's *A Raisin in the Sun* (1958), Brown's *Manchild in the Promised Land* (1965), Gregory's *Nigger* (1965), Thomas's *Down These Mean Streets* (1967), Rodriguez's *Hunger of Memory* (1982), Haley's *The Autobiography of Malcolm X* (1973), Chase-Riboud's historical novel *Sally Hemings* (1979), and many others.

I anticipated that these reading assignments could supplement the oral narratives and empower students, learners, and researchers by having them become knowledgeable about historical data during an era when civil rights for Blacks and other groups were not granted. These readings would also provide the opportunity for students to find some "entry" into these lives so that they could begin to better understand the narratives they had heard and were hearing and to understand the subjective experiences of these individuals. This method appears to have been helpful because as the learners presented oral highlights from the readings, they expressed that they attached new meanings to the term *oppressed*. For example, one learner, who expressed shock to learn that Thomas Jefferson owned slaves, clearly found some realm of entry into the life of the "slave" girl/woman Sally Hemings. She related to the powerlessness of Sally, who did not breast-feed her own babies because she did not want her breasts to sag, but when her master, Thomas Jefferson, died, her new mistress, Jefferson's sister, forced Sally to breast-feed her babies. This learner expressed her horror over the insensitivity of it all and began to realize what slavery must have felt like. She described how such demands took away Sally's pride, dignity, control of her own body, and even her soul.

Although these autobiographies provided a method for these adult learners to gain new knowledge, the oral histories that the learners heard provided them with firsthand insights: First, the powerlessness that the community exhibits can be considered "power absence" rather than "power failure" (Solomon, 1976, p. 21). Second, some negative valuations do not result in powerlessness because strong family relationships or strong cohesive group relationships provide a cushion from the larger society. For example, some Blacks and some of the other groups who shared oral histories with these learners were able to obtain and use a broad range of personal, interpersonal, and technical resources to achieve goals effectively.

Community members expressed extreme pleasure that the university used community resources and voiced a willingness to support any future efforts on behalf of my courses. In this venture, students, the community, and I were empowered through dialogue as each gained new respect and understanding of the other. During the next 6 years, I held classes in all of the ethnic communities mentioned earlier. New arrivals such as the Vietnamese, migrant workers, Haitians, and Native Americans also have shared parts of their history. I have learned, as have the community researchers, adult learners, and students, that an interdependence exists among all people. Both the tellers and the listeners are empowered by this exchange. Groups who have faced oppression have become the focus of my oral history research during the past 12 years and continue to inform the oral history research course I presently teach.

I have divided the book into two parts. In the five chapters of Part I, I define and trace the uses of oral history as qualitative research. Examples of narratives are included to demonstrate the many uses of oral history in shaping social reality and in building the knowledge base of the profession. I outline the multidimensional perspective that I use throughout my research to discover the adaptive strengths of individuals. I have included research on how others, including students, have used oral history to develop knowledge through the lenses of people who have been left out of the system. I define and describe an 11-step process used to conduct oral history and transcribe, edit, and analyze the results. I also draw parallels between the social work helping process and the skills of the oral history researcher.

In Part II, I present five examples of oral history research along with narratives and thoughts about their use. In a final chapter, I discuss the use of oral history as an intervention tool. The emphasis is on using oral histories in interpersonal, group, and community practice. I conclude the book with remarks on the inclusion of oral history for teaching, practice, and research. The purpose and value of the volume is to empower researchers, practitioners, educators, and other human service providers to embrace the oral history methodology.

NOTE

1. *Black* and *African American* are used interchangeably in this book.

REFERENCES

Angelou, M. (1970). *I know why the caged bird sings*. New York: Bantam.

Brown, C. (1965). *Manchild in the promised land*. New York: Macmillan.

Chase-Riboud, B. (1979). *Sally Hemings*. New York: Avon.

Gregory, D. (1965). *Nigger*. New York: Pocket.

Haley, A. (1973). *The autobiography of Malcolm X*. New York: Ballentine.

Hansberry, L. (1958). *A raisin in the sun*. New York: New American Library.

Rodriguez, R. (1982). *Hunger of memory: The education of Richard Rodriguez*. Boston: Godine.

Solomon, B. B. (1976). *Black empowerment: Social work in oppressed communities*. New York: Columbia University Press.

Thomas, P. (1967). *Down these mean streets*. New York: American Library.

Wright, R. (1945). *Black boy*. New York: Harper & Brothers.

PART I
Oral History in
Practice and Research

1

VALUING THE SUBJECTIVE EXPERIENCE
Oral History as Qualitative Research

> When I was a kid my greatest ambition was to go to college, and hurry up. All the young people were coming home from college and they used to have this dance they called the Return Student Ball. And all I wanted to do was hurry up and finish high school, go to college, come back and go to the Return Student Ball. . . . One day, I would be there. Something to inspire you. I can always remember when I was a small kid, all the way through, Dr. Bethune used to come to Tampa to speak, my mother would rush home from work, fix us dinner, we would dress and she would drag me to go hear Dr. Mary McLeod Bethune. I don't care how many times she came to Tampa, I had to go with my mama.

> Woman, age 73

You have just read excerpts from a tape-recorded interview with a Black woman who was born in the South in 1910. It is drawn from an oral history research project on Black family adaptation, survival, and growth that I conducted from 1982 through 1984. Her recounting of how she was able to eventually go to college and have a career as an educator provides insight into the ways Blacks have used individual and collective resources to adapt, survive, and grow in America. It is not a story that is often told.

In this chapter, I define and trace the uses of oral history. Through examples, I define the term *narrative* and acquaint readers with the process of planning a project and setting a time frame and goals. Finally, I present the rationale for using oral history in social work. I also discuss oral history from the point of view of other disciplines to emphasize the importance of oral history in providing a sense of continuity of life and information on the adaptive strengths of survivors. My purpose is to demonstrate the many uses of oral history for understanding individuals and groups as well as their perceptions of the forces that shape their social realities.

DEFINITION OF ORAL HISTORY

Baum (1970), who has written extensively on the techniques of transcribing and editing oral history, defines oral history as follows:

A way of taking down reminiscences by means of a tape recorder; not random reminiscences but planned interviews on a subject of historical interest about which the narrator can speak with authority. . . . [The interviewee] can be someone who was in an influential position at the time of the event . . . or an observation post . . . or articulate representative of a class of person . . . or old timer who can describe a past way of life.

ROOTS OF ORAL HISTORY

The use of oral history to transmit tradition was common to ancient Asian, Middle Eastern, and African cultures (Haley, 1976; Martin, 1991; Ong, 1977). In a recent discussion, Stave (personal communication, January 17, 1995) differentiates between oral history and oral tradition: "When I use the term *oral history*, I am referring to post-1948." Ong (1977) discusses oral history as beginning at the mother's knee, but he also describes its prominence as a way of transmitting tradition in "primitive" cultures (p. 21), a term that many African Americans and others find unacceptable. It is their view that Africa represented not "primitive cultures" but highly civilized societies that kept oral histories long before humans knew how to write. According to Ong, "such histories encourage a sense of continuity with life—a sense of participation because it [oral history] is itself participation" (p. 21). Haley (1976), a journalist who portrayed this sense of continuity by tracing his family's life history to Africa, covering seven generations, discovered the continued existence of *griots*—men who are walking archives in the older backcountry villages of Africa. Like Ong, Haley reflected on the ancient origins of oral history: "These Gambian men reminded me that every living person ancestrally goes back to some time and place when no writing existed, . . . when . . . human memories, mouths, and ears were the only way those human beings could store and relay information" (p. 574).

Blacks were "legally enjoined from being taught to read and write" for more than three centuries after having been brought to America (West,

1972, p. 3). It could be argued that much of what American Blacks have learned of a positive nature regarding their culture, resiliency, self-help techniques, and contributions to human civilization and American society was handed down in a like manner.

THE ORAL HISTORY PROJECT

The modern concept of oral history is generally attributed to Nevins, a celebrated history professor at Columbia University (see Starr, 1984). Nevins, whose work was geared only to the elite, interviewed well-known historical figures such as New York governors Nelson A. Rockefeller and Herbert H. Lehman and the jurist Learned Hand. Nevins (1966) lamented that with the invention of the telephone, "what might have been a priceless document for the historian goes into irrecoverable ether" (p. 600) because people may no longer bother to write and store letters and other written materials to review at a later time.

Rumic (1966), transcriber for the Oral History Research Office at Columbia University, described what has come to be known as an oral history project:

An oral history project comprises an organized series of interviews with selected individuals or groups in order to create new source materials from the reminiscences of their own life and acts or from association with a particular person, period or event. These recollections are recorded on tape and transcribed on typewriter into sheets of transcripts. (pp. 602-603)

An *oral history project* refers to an organized series of interviews with selected individuals or groups through which the participants tell their own life stories, in their own words, thereby creating new source material. In contrast, *oral history* refers to the whole process: interviewing, taping or recording, transcribing, editing, analyzing, interpreting, writing up the results, and making public the results. I touch on only some of the steps here and explain more thoroughly in Chapters 4 and 5.

ORAL NARRATIVES

Both the excerpt at the beginning of this chapter and the following interview I conducted with an 84-year-old African American widow are *oral narratives*. Oral narratives refer to the materials gathered in the oral history process using a tape recorder. I arrived at the widow's home by appointment one blistering summer afternoon, shortly after she had returned from a day at the office. The following transcript excerpt is at the beginning of the narrative phase of the interview when we were getting acquainted.

Narrator: When I came here [Tampa] we didn't have all this trouble with heat. Of course we had summer and winter, and now down here we don't even know the summer from the winter. Last year we didn't have much winter, it just stayed hot. Where I was raised we had snow, rain and freeze, the icicles on the trees freeze up and fall off.

Q: Where were you born in South Carolina?

N: I was born in Richmond County, South Carolina, out from Columbia. When I married, I was living in Columbia, and I came here straight from Columbia, 55 years ago, and I been here ever since. I came here to stay 3 months. My husband was transferred here on the job—he was working for the railroad, and I came to stay 3 months, and I haven't gone back yet to stay. I go back on visits.

Q: Uh huh.

N: When I first came here I said I didn't want nothing here, 'cause I didn't like nothing here and I didn't want to stay. But I just got tired paying rent, paying rent, paying rent, so I decided I would buy my own home and so I did. Purchasing a home, and then after purchasing a home, I purchased some property around and kept on building and so, that's where I am now.

Q: Uh huh. They tell me you manage a nursing home.

N: Yes.

Q: How did you come to own a nursing home?

N: By working in the hospital. I was a practical nurse and I worked in the hospitals. I worked everywhere and I worked from 16 to 24 hours a day, continual. Get off one job and go right on the other. I'm the mother of 10 children and I had to work and raise my family. . . . I had to educate my children. Their father died. He left before he died, but anyway he died. Left me with the bag to hold, and children don't have nobody but father and mother. And when their father don't do, mother got to do. So that's what I felt like I had to do. Now as far as opening a nursing home, I started taking people in my home and I didn't have a mind on opening a nursing home, but then the state asked me to open a nursing home because there wasn't any at that time. . . . I would take patients home when they were discharged and didn't have nowhere to go. I'd take them home and take care of them until they could reach relatives. Some of them were from out of town or different places. And the times wasn't like it is now. People weren't killing and stealing like they do now. So, I just felt the sympathy for everybody and I just took in people and took care of them the best I could. So then when I was asked to open a nursing home I refused to do it for a while, but after they told me I had been recommended, I've always been a person if somebody recommended me to do something I wouldn't let them down. I don't know where they found the confidence to recommend me, but they did it. I told them to wait until I pray over it. That's the way I do everything. Everything I have to do and everything I thought to do, everything I have in mind to do. I'm a devout churchgoer, and everything I have to do or I'm call on to do, I consult God about it: I pray over it. If the Lord directs me to go ahead, then I go ahead and do what's inevitable because he will help you with anything, if you trust him. All that's necessary is to put your trust in God, and have faith in, and know that he has already done what he said he would do. So, that's just the way it is. I started building and I worked, worked, worked, worked, worked. They laughed at me about working so hard, said I was grasping because I worked so, but I had my children to raise and I had to try and educate them. And I did pretty good at it. Me and Jesus, no one else.

I selected this narrative because it demonstrates how one might gain knowledge about adaptive capacities—in this case, those of an African American woman who was born in the latter part of the 19th century. Through the narrative, I attempted to use the skills of interviewing by beginning with what the participant wanted to talk about. The skill necessary to allow her to tell the story in her own words included both attentive listening and exploring. The interviewee shared how she took responsibility for others ("I took patients home from the hospital when they had no place to go"). This woman was not a social worker, but I was moved by how well she demonstrated the value base of the profession of social work, which is that individuals have social responsibility for each other. Her comment illustrates the interdependence between individuals in this society.

Information gained in an oral narrative interview is used to better understand but not to assess or form judgements about the interviewee, as would be the case in a diagnostic interview. This important difference frees both interviewer and interviewee to participate spontaneously in the process. But it is a disciplined spontaneity that requires knowing when to explore and when to listen. For example, note my exploratory comment as I questioned, "How did you come to own a nursing home?" and my active listening as I refrained from interrupting the interviewee and encouraged with "Uh huh."

RATIONALE FOR ORAL HISTORY IN SOCIAL WORK

Oral history has implications for social work practice in many areas. These include contribution to professional knowledge, values communication, development of skills that can also be used in assessment and intervention, and teaching methodology.

Stone (1977), a pioneer in oral history at the University of Connecticut, suggests four motives for conducting oral history: (a) obtaining information where little documentary evidence exists or where documentation is suspect; (b) revising history where its conclusions are suspect; (c) protecting against oblivion, such as loss of history; and (d) collecting phenomenological data, where most appropriate to illuminate the holistic nature of the subject's biopsychosocial functioning. Oral history is also useful as a supplement to other types of historical data, including erratic records and information from underrepresented or maligned groups. The importance of oral history to social workers is underscored as we consider our professional mandate to prioritize service to oppressed groups (Lee, 1994). These rationales for use of oral history are applicable to all helping professions. Medicine, for example, uses the life interview for the enhancement of clinical medicine and the elucidation of human development. Harris and Harris (1980) describe oral history as a "technique which enables the clinician, patient, and family to understand how the individual and family cope with health, illness, hopes and life as they age" (pp. 27-28). This view of oral history complements my own: that the value of oral history goes beyond gathering facts. It allows individuals and families to ascribe meaning to those events. When I described my research project on life forces of African American elderly to a participant, he responded, "In other words, you want to put meat on the bones." That is exactly what I was attempting to do (see Martin, 1991).

Oral history is especially useful in integrating humanistic values. Bennett (1983) notes that oral histories can be used to communicate across social barriers. Internal thoughts and feelings can be externalized only in language. Oral histories seem close to being experience itself and provide a picture of how experience is understood. A popular writer who makes extensive use of oral narratives is Terkel, author of *Hard Times* (1970), *Working* (1974), *American Dreams* (1980), and *The Good War* (1984). These books include examples of the effectiveness of oral history in conveying multiple perspectives and in illustrating the adaptation of diverse groups of "people who are being put down by the system, left out" (Terkel, quoted in Talcott, 1979, p. 461).

In his most recent work, *Race,* Terkel (1992) gets to the heart of the matter as both Blacks and Whites describe the subjective meaning of race as the American obsession. Terkel is a master of the oral narrative, and we can all learn a great deal from his technique. Terkel's work, however, is not entirely oral history. Hoopes (1979) has noted that Terkel's works are written from a journalistic perspective, heavily edited and shaped for the general public. Nevertheless, I have found it useful to suggest that practitioners invite discussion on many of the racial issues portrayed in Terkel's narratives and record them exactly as stated to gain an understanding of their clients' subjective experiences.

Within the profession of social work, Germain (1990), a prominent theoretician, speaks of "life forces" (p. 138), the unique course of events and varied life experiences each person encounters from birth through old age. Drawing on the work of Stern (1985), Germain notes that the sharing of "life stories" (p. 139) is crucial to the healing process. As human beings acquire language, they also begin spinning a life story about themselves and their relationship to the rest of the world. Germain builds a case for an inner narrative that at any given time can be accessed to provide insight into the individual's inner life. It is not necessary that the story begin with the earliest years or even that chronological order and other historic points be scrupulously maintained. The "truth" lurks in the patterns and connections between life events as revealed in the telling of the story. Thus oral history, which formalizes the storytelling process with the interviewer-social worker intervening as midwife, can provide a bridge between the problems social workers and their clients seek to confront and the clients' own solutions.

In addition, oral history methodology may be used with families whose functioning is nonproblematic. The interviewees who are selected need not be clients facing adversity or unresolved problems. They are often well-functioning individuals and families with good social and survival skills. Such resource material may provide knowledge to enhance practice interventions with those who do need help.

ORAL HISTORY AND CULTURAL DIVERSITY

In addition to generating professional knowledge and understanding of values, oral history can be used to help develop the skills of practitioners in working with culturally diverse populations. For example, Lewis's (1963) work demonstrates development of skills in relationship building, eliciting information, and intervention by being attuned to the interviewee's sense of time and space. As a result of professionals having developed these skills, "unskilled, uneducated, and even illiterate persons" can use their own words to "relate their observations and experiences," expressing their innermost feelings and depicting their very existence in "an uninhibited spontaneous and natural manner" (p. xii).

Social work has always recognized the importance of gathering and interpreting historical data about the families of people the profession serves. In *Social Diagnosis,* Richmond (1917) stressed the usefulness of social evidence and social diagnosis. She envisioned social evidence as supplementing the work of justice, healing, and teaching. Currently, the biopsychosocial history, constructivism, and use of the narrative are important trends in social work practice.

Published accounts of the use of oral history in social work include Bail's (1983) groups in nursing homes, Karminsky's (1984) reminiscence among older adults, and Solomon's (1976) assignment of oral history exercises to her students. Reissman (1987) presents two contrasting interviews with an Anglo woman and a Puerto Rican woman to demonstrate that an Anglo interviewer may not be able to make sense of a working-class Puerto Rican woman's account of her marital situation because of the way in which the story was told. In contrast, the Anglo social worker had little difficulty tuning in to an Anglo woman's chronological account of her marital separation. The two interviewees communicated their culturally distinctive marriage experience quite differently. Reissman concludes, "Applying narrative methods to these interviews shows how closer attention to the voice of the subject can enrich qualitative research" (p. 172).

More recently, Anderson and Jack (1991), a feminist social worker and a speech communication professor writing about oral history, demonstrate the value of learning to listen. They learned from each other as they shared and critiqued their interviews. The process helped them sharpen their listening skills and improve their interviewing methods.

The social work profession espouses a commitment to social justice and a respect for the worth of all individuals regardless of age, gender, race, class, or sexual orientation. Social workers also have an ethical responsibility for understanding and sensitivity in filling gaps in the chronology of minority group adaptation, survival, and growth. For example, because the Black family is so often portrayed as dysfunctional, understanding its adaptive structure, role, and functioning is particularly important (Billingsley, 1969; Logan, Freeman, & McRay, 1990). The unrecorded wealth of historical data about minority and subgroup survival can be retained through oral history. This information not only can interpret the past for the present generation but also can provide a broader knowledge base for future generations and the motivation to work to prevent perpetuation of "racial degradation, exploitation, and segregation" (R. R. Martin, 1987, p. 7).

Terry's *Bloods* (1984) exemplifies the use of oral history to allow 20 Black Vietnam War veterans to share their meaning of the war and to supplement historical gaps. Tollefson (1993) adds another viewpoint to military history in *The Strength Not to Fight: An Oral History of Conscientious Objectors of the Vietnam War.* He allows these men to tell of the strength it took to take their stances in the face of family objections, persecution, and criminal prosecution. Shiltz (1987) also captures the politics and history of AIDS in the gay male community partly through the use of oral narratives in the now classic *And the Band Played On.*

Oral history reveals the human diversities in the Black experience by documenting differences among subcultures in coping techniques and reactions to racism. It also broadens awareness of the interdependence among family, community, and political systems and underscores the psychological forces of the wider society that impinge on the Black family and the quality of family life. For example, Hampton and Fayer (1990), in the prologue of their *Voices of Freedom: An Oral History of the Civil Rights Movement From the 1950s Through the 1980s,* describe through narratives "a moment in American history when the country was forced to decide whether it would live up to its principles, people who pushed the country to change, and the voices of those who resisted" (p. xxiii). At the same time, oral history emphasizes the fundamental human experience, as Solomon (1976) suggests: "Black families, like Black individuals, are like all other families in the United States, like some other families, and like no other families all at the same time" (p. 181). Comer (1988), a professor of child psychiatry at the Yale University Child Study Center, recounts his own family experience. He compares the example of "five college-educated children of parents undereducated and from low-income backgrounds with that of friends from the same background who were just as intelligent but whose lives had less desirable outcomes" (p. xxiii). He theorizes that such an example points to "critical differences that go beyond racial issues alone . . . stories that are not being told by scholars and media obsessed with the victims" (p. xxiii).

Pinderhughes (1983), a renowned social work educator and the great-granddaughter of a slave, researched her family's story back to the time of slavery in Louisiana and Mississippi and found it a therapeutic experience. She expressed having achieved an expanded appreciation of her personal continuity with history and time, similar to the experience reported by Ong (1977). Drawing on Walker's (1983) *In Search of Our Mothers' Gardens,* Miller (1990) writes about the importance of continuity for life: "For the sake of their children, every people must collect 'bone by bone' the genius of their past family stories, [and] memories, give order to and continuity in a swirling social universe" (p. 8).

Other minority groups of color who have been left out tell important stories about their family values, religious rituals and beliefs, and historic experiences through use of oral histories. For example, Hong-Kingston uses oral history in *China Men* (1980) and *The Woman Warrior* (1976). Social workers can draw on this knowledge for social work practice. Oral history told to social work students in a course I taught provided them an opportunity to gain new knowledge and perceptions about families who left Cuba before Fidel Castro came to power and those who left after he became leader. Immigrant workers, Cubans (both Black and White), Puerto Ricans, Native Americans, and Vietnamese refugees provided students with new knowledge about each group's struggles to overcome poverty, social isolation, social injustice, and hostilities. The immigrants described the difficulties of their transaction in a nonnutritive environment and described their coping, adaptation, and mastery. The class also learned what meanings different cultures apply to the same events.

Wall and Arden (1990) discuss the importance of face-to-face interviews with Native American wisdom keepers. They write, "We are changed. We have been seized and shaken. We went out two journalists after a good story. We came back two 'runners' from another world, carrying an urgent message from the Wisdom Keepers" (p. 10). White Deer of Autumn (1990) in Wall and Arden writes in his editorial notes: "Reading the words of the Wisdom Keepers, we must understand that these terms—God, Creators, and Great Spirit—have been used to convey the concept that all things are interrelated and an equal part of the whole" (p. 5).

In *New Americans: An Oral History,* a book on immigration, Santoli (1988) allows a multicultural group of people, including Asians, Latins, Africans, Moslems, Jews, and Slavs, to tell stories that appear to reach to the core of their being. The immigrants' sharing of their experiences and subjective reality gives historians, policymakers, and community leaders working with these new Americans a better understanding of who they are. Stave and Sutherland (1994) provide insight into the immigrant experience in *From the Old Country: An Oral History of European Migration to America.* They draw on the series of interviews with immigrants and their children conducted by the Works Progress Administration (WPA) Ethnic Group Survey conducted from 1938 through 1940 in Connecticut, as well as in other states. They also use their own material gathered during the 1970s and 1980s. In this way, they cover nearly a century of reflections about the immigrant experience.

Anthropologist Myerhoff's (1978) *Number Our Days* is an ethnographic study of impoverished elderly Jewish immigrants who came to America at the turn of the century and now live at the edge of the Pacific

Ocean in Venice, California, where they retired after years of work in the garment industry. Her work depicts them in old age, experiencing difficult life problems and issues of geographic separation from children, poverty, declining health, and social isolation—but resilient and surviving. At the time of her death, Myerhoff (1988), in an unfinished article, *Surviving Stories: Reflection on Number Our Days,* writes, "Twelve years later, they have not died out. From the beginning, their circumstances were more burdened and imperiled than ever. All stories of surviving are miracle tales, and theirs are no different" (p. 19).

In addition to its importance for selected ethnic and racial groups, oral history provides new knowledge for another group: women. It is also a method most appropriate to the unique experience of those women who do not write and who are the keepers of the family story. Gluck (1984) espouses that women are refusing to be rendered historically voiceless and are thereby creating a new history through use of their own voices and experience. She sees women reconstructing their own past, challenging the traditional concept of history, redefining what is historically important, and forcing others to recognize that women's everyday lives are indeed history.

Sarah and Elizabeth Delaney (1993), whose father was born into slavery, tell their story in *Having Our Say.* These sisters, 100 and 103 at the time of the book's publication, share stories of Jim Crow and legal segregation, the World War I era, their migration north, and their rise to professional prominence in the heyday of Harlem. One is at once impressed and awed by the strengths of these physically fragile but fiercely independent women, as they live alone in their own home without a telephone, making peach preserves and soap. They are up-to-date on current events, and yes, to be reckoned with.

Nevins and Perlstein (1984) discuss oral histories of women via audiovisual films. For example, one film depicts the changing role of women in the 20th century, whereas another features four women from Mississippi who describe the nature and evolution of their different art forms. These films are able to give the audience insight into their lives, into the "something" that "shapes people" (p. 328). Berzon (1979) does this in the coming out stories of lesbian women presented in *Positively Gay.*

The richness of the oral history methodology helps social work practitioners understand the "something" that shapes the lives of the people with whom social workers practice and empower. For example, Winkler (1991) reports on Sherbakova's (1991) research on Soviet labor camps, which she presented at the annual meeting of the Oral History Association. In oral history interviews with 300 women, Sherbakova recorded life in the

Gulag from 1918 to 1953. She tells of the estimated 20 million people who were arrested during that period. Most of the survivors were women and were not released until after the death of Joseph Stalin in 1953. Sherbakova told Winkler that although the Soviet regime considered memories to be dangerous, the old people who had been in the camps could not forget.

V. B. Martin's (1987) "A Study in Black and White: An Oral History of Hartford's First Year of Busing and How It Changed Fifteen Lives" presents some of the problems of an innovative school integration busing program. Martin interviewed Blacks and Whites who, looking back 20 years, told of the difficulties of this program and issues they still face today, such as limited experiences outside of their respective racial groups. The study was used in history and civic classrooms as an educational tool from elementary through graduate school.

In his book *The Making of Urban History: Historiography Through Oral History,* Stave (1979) uses oral history to interview several leading practitioners of urban history. Stave and Sutherland (1985/1990), in *Talking About Connecticut: Oral History in the Nutmeg State,* recount: "The new social history, as it came to be known, was a people's history. And who knew more about the people than they themselves? . . . By interviewing the un-famous, we learned much about the immigrant experience, family history, women's history, neighborhoods, workers and other similar topics" (p. 3). Stave and Sutherland's oral history of Connecticut was enthusiastically received, and the demand for workshops and training sessions in public schools, historical societies, and libraries continues, showing the broad and enduring educational value of oral history.

CONCLUSION

In this chapter, I have discussed how social workers and other professionals, practitioners, and individuals can use the oral history method to produce data that portray the subjective experience of individuals. I outlined the rationale for its use as a research methodology for integrating minority, gender, multicultural, ethnic, racial, and subcultural content in social work education. I presented an oral interview and showed how I gained knowledge of strengths and the continuity of life for various groups of people.

In Chapter 2, I discuss oral history in social work service and education and show how oral history, like other forms of qualitative research, can be used for learning about differences, for community education, for staff development in agencies, for assessment and program planning, and with client populations to promote involvement and empowerment. I place special emphasis on giving voice to the voiceless.

REFERENCES

Anderson, K., & Jack, D. C. (1991). *Learning to listen: Interview techniques and analysis.* In S. B. Gluck & D. Patai (Eds.), *Women's words: The feminist practice of oral history* (pp. 11-26). New York: Routledge, Chapman & Hall.

Bail, M. (1983). Oral histories: A nursing home project. *Practice Digest, 6,* 7-8.

Baum, W. K. (1970, October). *Oral history for the local historical society.* Presentation at a seminar of the Oral History Association, Harrisburg, PA.

Bennett, J. (1983). Human values in oral history. *The Oral History Review, 2,* 1-15.

Berzon, B. (1979). Telling the family you're gay. In R. Leighton (Ed.), *Positively gay* (pp. 67-78). Millbrae, CA: Celestial Arts.

Billingsley, A. (1969). Family functioning in the low-income Black community. *Social Casework, 50,* 563-572.

Comer, J. P. (1988). *Maggie's American dream.* New York: New American Library.

Delaney, S., & Delaney, A. E. (with Hearth, A. H.). (1993). *Having our say: The Delaney sisters' first 100 years.* New York: Kodansha America.

Germain, C. B. (1990). Life forces and the anatomy of practice. *Smith College Studies in Social Work, 60*(2), 138-152.

Gluck, S. (1984). What's so special about women? Women's oral history. In D. K. Dunway & W. K. Baum (Eds.), *Oral history: An interdisciplinary anthology* (pp. 221-237). Nashville, TN: American Association for State and Local History.

Haley, A. (1976). *Roots: The saga of an American family.* New York: Doubleday.

Hampton, H., & Fayer, S. (1990). *Voices of freedom: An oral history of the civil rights movement from the 1950s through the 1980s.* New York: Bantam.

Harris, R., & Harris, S. (1980). Therapeutic uses of oral history techniques in medicine. *International Journal of Aging and Human Development, 12*(1), 27-33.

Hong-Kingston, M. (1976). *The woman warrior.* South Yarmouth, MA: J. Curley.

Hong-Kingston, M. (1980). *China men.* New York: Knopf.

Hoopes, J. (1979). *Oral history: An introduction for students.* Chapel Hill: University of North Carolina Press.

Karminsky, M. (Guest Ed.). (1984). The uses of reminiscence: New ways of working with older adults [Special issue]. *Journal of Gerontological Social Work, 7*(1-2).

Lee, J. A. B. (1994). *The empowerment approach to social work practice.* New York: Columbia University Press.

Lewis, O. (1963). *The children of Sanchez: Autobiography of a Mexican family.* New York: Random House.

Logan, S., Freeman, E., & McRay, R. (1990). *Social work practice with Black families.* New York: Longman.

Martin, R. R. (1987). Oral history in social work education: Chronicling the Black experience. *Journal of Social Work Education, 23*(3), 5-10.

Martin, R. R. (1991, August 23-25). *Life forces of African American elderly illustrated through oral history narratives.* Paper presented at a conference on Qualitative Methods in Social Work Research Practice, State University of New York at Albany, School of Social Welfare, Nelson A. Rockefeller Institute of Government.

Martin, V. B. (1987, February 1). A study in Black and White: An oral history of Hartford's first year of busing and how it changed fifteen lives. *Northeast* [Hartford *Courant* Sunday magazine], pp. 8-28.

Miller, R. M. (Ed.). (1990). *Dear master: Letters of a slave family.* Athens: University of Georgia Press.

Myerhoff, B. (1978). *Number our days.* New York: Simon & Schuster.

Myerhoff, B. (1988). Surviving stories: Reflections on number our days. *Tikkun, 2*(5), 19-25.

Nevins, A. (1966). Oral history: When and why it was born. *Wilson Library Bulletin, 40*(7), 600-601.

Nevins, A., & Perlstein, S. (1984). Oral histories of women. *The Gerontologist, 24*(3), 328-332.

Ong, W. J. (1977). *Interface of the word: Studies in the evolution of consciousness and culture.* New York: Cornell University Press.

Pinderhughes, E. (1983). Empowerment for our clients and for ourselves. *Social Casework, 64,* 331-338.

Richmond, M. (1917). *Social diagnosis.* New York: Russell Sage.

Riessman, C. K. (1987). When gender is not enough: Women interviewing women. *Gender & Society, 1*(2), 172-207.

Rumic, E. (1966). Oral history: Defining the term. *Wilson Library Bulletin, 40*(7), 602-603.

Santoli, A. (1988). *New Americans: An oral history: Immigrants and refugees in the U.S. today.* New York: Ballantine.

Sherbakova, I. (1991, October). [Life in the gulag.] Research presented at the annual meeting of the Oral History Association, Snowbird, UT.

Shiltz, R. (1987). *And the band played on: Politics, people and the AIDS epidemic.* New York: St. Martin's.

Solomon, B. B. (1976). *Black empowerment: Social work in oppressed communities.* New York: Columbia University Press.

Starr, L. M. (1984). Oral history. In D. K. Dunway & W. K. Baum (Eds.), *Oral history: An interdisciplinary anthology* (pp. 4-26). Nashville, TN: American Association for State and Local History.

Stave, B. M. (1979). *The making of urban history: Historiography through oral history.* Beverly Hills, CA: Sage.

Stave, B. M., & Sutherland, J. F. (Eds.). (1990). *Talking about Connecticut: Oral history in the Nutmeg State* (Rev. ed.). Storrs: University of Connecticut, Center for Oral History and Manchester Community College, Institute of Local History. (Original work published 1985)

Stave, B. M., & Sutherland, J. F. (with Salerno, A.). (1994). *From the old country: An oral history of European migration to America.* New York: Twane.

Stern, D. (1985). *The interpersonal world of the infant.* New York: Basic Books.

Stone, F. A. (1977). *Using oral history in educational studies* (Multicultural Research Guides Series, No. 1). Storrs: University of Connecticut, Isaac Newton Thut World Education Center.

Talcott, W. (1979). Organizer: An interview with Studs Terkel. In F. M. Cox, J. L. Erlich, J. Rothman, & J. E. Tropman (Eds.), *Studies of community organizations: A book of readings* (3rd ed., pp. 461-464). Itasca, IL: F. E. Peacock.

Terkel, S. (1970). *Hard times: An oral history of the great depression.* New York: Pantheon.

Terkel, S. (1974). *Working: People talk about what they do all day and how they feel about what they do.* New York: Pantheon.

Terkel, S. (1980). *American dreams: Lost and found.* New York: Ballantine.

Terkel, S. (1984). *The good war: An oral history of World War II.* New York: Ballantine.

Terkel, S. (1992). *Race: How Blacks and Whites think and feel about the American obsession.* New York: New Press.

Terry, W. (1984). *Bloods: An oral history of the Vietnam War by Black veterans.* New York: Random House.

Tollefson, J. W. (1993). *The strength not to fight: An oral history of conscientious objectors of the Vietnam War.* Boston: Little, Brown.

Walker, A. (1983). *In search of our mothers' gardens: Womanist prose.* San Diego, CA: Harcourt Brace Jovanovich.

Wall, S., & Arden, H. (1990). *Wisdom keepers: Meetings with American spiritual elders.* Hillsboro, OR: Beyond Words.

West, E. H. (1972). *The Black American and education.* Columbus, OH: Merrill.

White Deer of Autumn. (1990). Editorial notes. In S. Wall & H. Arden (Eds.), *Wisdom keepers: Meetings with American spiritual elders* (pp. 4-5). Hillsboro, OR: Beyond Words.

Winkler, K. J. (1991, October 30). Opening a window on life in Soviet labor camps. *Chronicle of Higher Education,* pp. A8, A12.

2

USING THEORETICAL
PERSPECTIVES FOR ORAL
HISTORY RESEARCH IN SOCIAL
WORK AND SOCIAL WORK EDUCATION

ORAL HISTORY IN SOCIAL WORK:
A MULTIDIMENSIONAL PERSPECTIVE

Theories, or frames of reference, are necessary to inform and enhance people's innate sensitivities, intuitions, and hunches. They also encourage reflective and penetrating questions that deepen understanding (Goldstein, 1990).

The theoretical bases I find useful in doing oral history for research purposes draw from field psychology (Lewin, 1951); the ecological perspective (Germain, 1979); the life model (Germain & Gitterman, 1980); and the dual perspective (Norton, 1978). When focusing on ethnic groups, I also draw on concepts used to explain and interpret the experience of those groups. For example, I often focus on the strengths of Black families (Hill, 1972; Logan, Freeman, & McRay, 1990); the Black family as a social system (Billingsley, 1968); and Black language (Draper, 1979). A brief overview of these theories and concepts follows.

FORCE FIELD ANALYSIS

Lewin's (1951) concept of life space force field analysis focuses on an individual's attempt to obtain certain goals and the driving or restraining

18

forces that may restrict movement toward these goals. These concepts also apply to organizational and institutional goals. His concept of *barriers* is useful because barriers—whether racial, political, social, economical, sexual, or educational—that are faced by oppressed people have restricted their movement toward their goals. In working with Black families and other people who have been left out of the system, social workers and other professionals need to determine the position of persons within their particular life space to assess the effect of barriers on functioning and adaptation.

The following narratives depict how I use selected theories to guide my research on African Americans' struggle to transcend restrictive forces. In the narrative below, an elderly gentleman describes oppressive conditions in the labor force:

> We were denied so many things that normally you would not know about unless someone told you. In fact, many Black kids don't know today the hassle that we had, if I should call it that, in arriving at the equalization of facilities, and salaries particularly. There are people in the school system today who do not know anything about the background. In 1940, the Black teacher was making 51% of the salary that was given to the White. It doesn't take a genius to realize what a tremendous disadvantage that was to us along with the fact that the salary for Whites was extremely low. I am saying low in terms of what the other part of the nation was getting at that time.
>
> They said the Black does not require the amount of learning as the White. So, if you increase Blacks' salaries, automatically the Whites will be lowered. At that time, I was one of only four in the county, either White or Black, who held a master's degree. (interview, January 18, 1983)

Lewin's (1951) theory tells me to look out for barriers, the oppressive forces in the environment. But he also recognizes the potential to reach goals by the use of driving forces as described in the narrative above.

THE ECOLOGICAL PERSPECTIVE

Two useful concepts flow from Germain's (1979) ecological perspective, which discusses people in relationship to environments (physical and social). The first is the "adaptive capacities" (p. 16) of people and the second is the "nutritive" (p. 16) qualities of the environment to emphasize goodness of fit, which enables them to adapt, grow, develop, cope, and "achieve reproductive success" (p. 8). The concepts of social pollutions, such as racism, sexism, and the abuse of power, are also important.

I apply force field analysis and the ecological perspective concepts to all of my research. For example, the following narrative from a female respondent born in 1903, who was the plaintiff in the suit for equalization of salary, portrays the effects of discrimination on self-identity and the maturational process. It also demonstrates that the African American community came together for the good of all. Perhaps they embraced the traditional African law and philosophy: "We, and not the I, is the law of African life" (Blyden, 1908, p. 30). As summarized by Mbiti (1970), this means, "I am because we are, and since we are, therefore I am" (p. 14). The former teacher and the community won the suit in a supportive effort. She recalls,

> Yes, we won. Two years later, after having taught 16 years in the system, I left and went to Chicago. I took a job substitute teaching. Since I changed from teaching high school to elementary school, I was required to take two courses on elementary school methods. For a permanent job, I was required to take a state teachers exam. I was afraid I couldn't pass. One lady talked with me, encouraging me, told me she was certain I could pass. I took the exam and made a score of 96. Next I had to take the oral examination. The lady encouraged and advised me. "When you go in, if you don't know the answer, just say you don't know. And don't sit until they ask you to." When I finished the oral, the chair of the group told me, "You have passed." I walked into that hall, walking on air, and it appeared as though the floor was rising up to meet me. (interview, January 12, 1984)

The narrator has demonstrated that given the opportunities and encouragement, she was able to reach a level of mastery and competence. She has now retired and returned home because as she said, "Family is always there for you" (interview, January 12, 1984). This theme of families helping families was consistent throughout the research with African American elderly. The strong kinship bond identified by Hill (1972) and the shared "sense of peoplehood" expressed by Billingsley (1968, p. 10) guide me as I apply the theoretical base of my research.

The former school teacher, who at the time of this writing is 90, continues to strive for competence. At 80, when I first interviewed her, she had said, "I have not heard the 2-minute whistle" (a phrase she explained is used in football). She was taking care of a great-nephew. When I listened to the tape of the interview, I was immediately tuned in to the patience displayed as she responded to a child who was physically challenged. It was not surprising to learn that she spent 25 years teaching the educable mentally retarded. She sums up her physical decline this way: "I feel blessed. I am perfectly healthy except for the surgery for cataracts. If it's corrected and I can see, I'll be happy. If the sight is not corrected, I will still feel blessed" (interview, January 12, 1984). In a special *Tampa Tribune* report on the progress of race relations, reporter Hawes (1991) recounted this woman's fight for equal pay and noted how her education continues: "She has had to resume the educational process herself. Because of dwindling eyesight, she has had to learn how to read and write braille" (p. 6).[1]

THE LIFE MODEL

I used the Germain and Gitterman (1980) life model to understand this participant's personal strengths and what social and physical resources she was able to find in her environment that enabled her to be so resilient. I am using theory to look for personal, social, and environmental strengths that she put together to overcome life's adversities. In addition, because much of my research is about African American families, I include theory that relates to the African American experience specifically and other minority groups generally. As Germain (1979) notes, American Blacks have developed a variety of adaptive behaviors as they struggle with issues of identity formation, autonomy, competence, and relatedness to others as well as in the development and maintenance of social network communication paths, relational linkages, systems of mutual aid, self-help groups, and natural helpers.

I use the life model framework (Germain & Gitterman, 1980) in my research to understand the meaning in the oral narratives. I selected this framework because it provides a transactional view that incorporates human diversity (race, ethnicity, gender, culture, sexual orientation, and physical and mental disability) as well as environmental diversity (economic, political, and social).

Goldstein (1990) suggests that the questions of "whether the knowledge base of social work comprises theory, wisdom, analogues, or art" (p. 33) should lead to the "nature of human purpose" (p. 38). Germain and Gitterman's (1980) model of social work practice is well suited because the social purpose calls for a practice method that is designed to engage people's strength and the forces pushing toward growth and to influence organizational structures, other social systems, and physical settings so they will be more responsive to people's needs.

Stress is another key concept taken from the life model. Germain and Gitterman (1980) argue that stress is a psychosocial condition generated by discrepancies between needs and capacities on one hand and environmental qualities on the other. They describe how stress arises in three interrelated areas of living: life transitions, environmental negotiations, and interpersonal processes. Life transitions might include, for example, changes that occur developmentally, as in adolescent pregnancy and the status and role changes from student to motherhood, from the roles of good student, daughter, and sister to the roles of breadwinner and caretaker. In Chapter 9, I present my research on adolescent mothers using these concepts to guide my work.

Germain and Gitterman (1980) hold that all life transitions require changes in self-image, in ways of looking at the world, in processing of information derived from cognition, in perception and feeling, in patterns of relating to others, in use of environmental resources, and in goals. All require the restructuring of a person's life, new adaptive behavior patterns, and new coping skills. Environmental nutrients are needed to help the adolescent mothers in Chapter 9 make the life transition to motherhood and to assist the transition to American life for the young Russian Jewish émigré, Slava, whose experiences are discussed in Chapter 7.

Unresponsive environments can be a source of great stress. For example, when the opportunity structure is closed to African Americans because of race, to Slava because of anti-Semitic political policies, and to other groups because of class, gender, sexual orientation, or age, adaptive capacities may be blocked. Organizations deigned to meet adaptive needs, that is, schools, welfare organizations, hospitals, and mental health centers, may also impose stress through unresponsive policies and procedures (Germain & Gitterman, 1980).

Relatives, friends, or neighbors may be absent or unresponsive or may not understand the importance of goal setting, as Betty, an adolescent mother whom I discuss more fully in Chapter 9, claims in discussing the lack of support by her siblings when she attempted to finish high school. Betty said, "It was hard living at home. My sisters complained about the baby . . . [crying] and different things." People may not have knowledge of what helping organizations might offer. They may lack political savvy to challenge the system when faced with poor economic conditions, overcrowded housing, lack of job opportunities, and other hazards. In other cases, knowledgeable others may be present and supportive (Martin, 1991, 1994).

In addition to life transitions and environmental unresponsiveness, stress may be experienced because of relationship patterns within the group itself. These maladaptive processes may include inconsistent expectations from practitioners and researchers and exploitative relationships and poor communications between individuals, within families, within peer groups such as female and male adolescents, and among the groups and service providers.

ADAPTIVE STRENGTHS

Draper (1979), another proponent of the ecological perspective, described other coping patterns that are reflective of Black adaptive strengths, such as strong primary supports of extended family networks (i.e., natural grandparents and "aunts," an affectionate title that may or may not connote genetic ties), strong church involvement, sense of fatalism (which is not always negative because this day-to-day quality contributes to survival), the ability to go to a good neighbor and ask for a few dollars or for child care while going to the clinic, and even the eternal hope of hitting the "number" in some urban communities. Draper also noted that Black language, music, and humor display adaptive strategies. According to Draper,

> It did not take the Black slaves long to understand that whatever they said to their white masters, or even to each other, must have . . . double meanings, . . . half truths, . . . other forms that would ensure their own personal safety. They quickly became adept at such survival mechanisms . . . learned to use the complete inventory of speech . . . (e.g., the range from the soft-spoken "mumbling word" to the hostile, loud aggressive distancing associated with white's image of the so-called "hostile Black male"), gesture and facial expression (impassive) to produce whatever appearance would be acceptable and life saving. (p. 276)

Norton's (1978) dual perspective helps explain the adaptive capacities of individuals who have been left out but who are operating in two systems:

> The nurturing system, which includes the family and immediate community environment and culture of an individual, and the sustaining system, which includes the organization of goods and services, political power, economic resources, and educational system, and larger societal systems. According to this perspective if there are broad areas of incongruence between the two systems, then individuals are prone to difficulties in functioning. Such individuals will have special needs. (p. 3)

Chestang (1979) also speaks of this biculturality as adaptive. This perspective helps to view the clients' responses in the context of their social environment.

Hill (1972) emphasizes the family as the critical unit of attention. He identifies five strengths of Black families and takes the view that Blacks have used many adaptive qualities, including strong kinship bonds, a strong work orientation, adaptability of family roles, a strong achievement orientation, and a strong religious orientation.

In Chapter 1, I introduced an 84-year-old African American woman. Not only does she drive herself to work every day, but until the year before our interview, she took the continuing education courses needed to renew her license to work with patients in the nursing home. She has 33 grandchildren. Although her grown children have their own homes, they still spend much time with her. "We are together, in an' out of each other's homes, night and day." I learned about this woman's children's and grandchildren's occupations as I was shown albums relating to family functions and describing relationships.

Billingsley (1968) also focuses on the family as the unit of attention as well as on other salient subsystems within the Black community. Among these subsystems are local small businesses, barber and beauty shops, fraternal organizations, grocery stores, churches, and streetcorner hustling. The macrosocial system approach by Billingsley, which focuses on family, community, and the wider society, portrays a vivid picture of subsystems of the Black community through which one is able to achieve better knowledge of the adaptive potentials of the Black families. Historical experiences are recognized and expressed through "a sense of peoplehood" (p. 10)—a shared sense of culture, language, and characteristics.

I have connected all of the previous theories into a repertoire of planned questions, which I will discuss more thoroughly in Chapter 3. I do not write my interview questions out as such but instead follow the flow of the interview. The blend of these perspectives forms the multidimensional framework for this book.

KNOWLEDGE BUILDING

Oral history methodology, as used in this volume, has similarities to the case study approach. Both seek to collect and examine data regarding the subject in environmental context. For oral history, this includes the personal recollections of the events, causes, effects of the participant's adaptive potential, and the environment's nutritive qualities that enable the participant to survive, develop, and succeed—as well as recollections of environmental obstacles. Both the case study and oral history rely on the interviewing skills of the researcher and the ability to establish trust with the participant and to use flexible, open-ended data collection and analysis techniques (Grinnell, 1981). Both are time-consuming and expensive, and flexible analysis techniques often present problems in coding. They differ, however, in that oral history methodology relies heavily on the snowball technique in which one interviewee identifies another. This technique is explained more fully in Chapter 4.

GROUNDED THEORY

Another method of qualitative research that aids in oral history is grounded theory, originally developed by Glaser and Strauss (1967). In a personal history of its development, Strauss (1991) writes,

> Grounded theory is inductively derived from the study of the phenomenon it represents. . . . It is discovered, developed, and provisionally verified through systematic data collection and analysis of data pertaining to that phenomenon. The three, data collection, analysis and theory, stand in reciprocal relationship with each other. One does not begin with a theory, then prove it. Rather, one begins with an area of study and what is relevant to that area is allowed to emerge. (pp. 1-2)

Using these principles in conducting oral history allows the researcher to begin with the interviewee and develop an understanding of the interviewee's subjective experience as the story unfolds. I also use the stance of the participant observer. Participant observation constitutes a distinct method itself, one that characterizes all field studies in anthropology (Bruyn, 1966).

PARTICIPANT OBSERVATION

Kluckhohn's definition of participant observation is derived from her fieldwork in a Mexican village. She describes participant observation as "conscious and systematic sharing, insofar as circumstances permit, in the life activities, and on occasion, in the interests and affects of a group of persons" (quoted in Bruyn, 1966, pp. 13-14). While working on an oral history project, I attended a church service honoring women of the community. I decided to videotape the program from the church's loft. As the choir sang some of the old Negro spirituals, I was moved almost to tears. When the choir sang the Negro National Anthem, I found myself joining them in singing. Not until I played back the tape did I realize how much more a participant than a distant observer I had become. Having been close to the microphone, my voice carried louder than the choir's!

I have come to share the view of Bruyn (1966), who realized that as a participant observer, he was studying "not human behavior so much as the inner collective life of people who were deeply involved personally in changing their community and in being changed by it" (p. x). This inner life revealed itself symbolically in the dialogues between people on street corners, in committees, in back rooms, and in assemblies. It, he argued, had visible counterparts in the statue on the square, the cemetery, and the new industry moving into or indeed, out of the community, leaving devastation and poverty. I came to recognize, as did Bruyn, that the

> evidence of this life generally appeared . . . not very conducive to the methods of a scientists' aiming for prediction, precision, and control. . . . It might be better for a novelist or a playwright to represent subtleties . . . of these terms in community life. . . . The social scientist must apprehend the original meanings of these terms with all their subtleties, for they were clearly a part of what was determining the course of social action. (p. x)

Through the use of oral history, social workers, educators, practitioners, and other learners can uncover what their behavior and life events *mean* to the people who provide them with information. Oral history is about meanings as well as events. Generating and using oral history in social work practice make it possible to view the clients' reality through the clients' cultural and experiential lenses and to participate, if vicariously, in their myths and rituals. Oral history sensitizes social workers to various cultural and generational perspectives by helping them understand another era, age group, social class, gender identity, and an ethnic pattern of meaning. Understanding comes from viewing the clients' experience through their cultural lenses.

The challenge is even greater. To truly understand the others, practitioners must view their *own* culture, myths, and rituals as well as age, era, social class, and region as illustrated through the lens of the other. This is good training for social workers because understanding the clients' interpretation of the world is the defining characteristic of social work (England, 1986). The difference, of course, is that oral history researchers help people express meaningful events (which may be cathartic in itself), whereas social workers explore the meaning of the events described with clients and at times intervene to make changes that clients desire.

It is often difficult to hear what people share in oral narratives. Langer (1991), writing about narratives of Holocaust survivors, suggests the following:

> Competent presentation and substantial contact will rouse and hold an audience's interest . . . but the first effect of many of these testimonies is just the opposite, no matter how vivid the presentation: they induce fear, confusion, shame, horror, skepticism, even disbelief. The more painful, dramatic, and overwhelming the narrative, the more tense, wary, and self protective is the audience, the quicker the instinct to withdraw. Unlike the writer, the witness here lacks inclination and strategies to establish and maintain a viable bond between the participants in this encounter. (p. 20)

I have noticed this same withdrawal in students during the discussion of oppression of racial minorities. When I asked a colleague why students became uncomfortable and self-protective and appeared almost threatened, he likened it to being invited to a big feast and afterwards being shown pictures of starving children in Third World countries. One feels guilty and ashamed of having been fed while others starve.

To reverse the direction of that initial estrangement, Langer (1991) contends that a viewer must find some entry into the realm of disrupted lives and become sensitized to the implications of such disruption. He believes that we have no choice but to come to the encounter unprepared. Nor can one approach the experience from the reservoir of normal values, armed with questions such as, "Why didn't they resist?" and "Why didn't they help one another?" Writes Langer, "The first answer is that they did; the second is that sometimes it made no difference; and the third is that, under those circumstances, more often than not they couldn't" (pp. 20-21). The same holds true for people oppressed through slavery and other abusive circumstances. By focusing on the meaning and on the respondent's own interpretation of the oral narrative, it is possible for the researcher to concentrate on the strengths and coping skills it takes to resist, the adaptive strengths it takes to endure, and the resilience it takes to bounce back.

BENEFITS OF ORAL HISTORY
TO SOCIAL WORK EDUCATION

In my own work, I have found that oral histories can be used for strengthening the knowledge base of social work education. I use oral histories to fill gaps in the knowledge base relative to three areas of minority and subgroup life: what has not been told, what has been told but only from a pathological view, and what has been only partially told. Oral histories are of value in expanding social workers' comprehension of the uniqueness of individual, cultural, and value orientations.

In my research, I prefer to use the term *research topic* or *issues* rather than to focus on *problems* to be studied because the oral history methodology may be used with persons and families whose functioning is nonproblematic. Participants need not be facing adversity or unresolved problems but are often well-functioning persons with good social and adaptive skills. In Chapters 6 through 10, I will present full examples of oral history research.

A MASTER'S LEVEL SOCIAL
WORK CLASS: ORAL HISTORY PROJECTS

Several years ago, I developed and taught an oral history research course designed to meet a curriculum requirement for students to implement a research study. The focus was on doing applied research that builds knowledge cumulatively. The class members were free to select the research topic. They chose "An Ecological Look at African American Elderly." Participants reasoned that a retrospective look at the African American elderly would increase their understanding of elderly persons' life courses, including how they coped with adversity and what environmental factors influenced their lives. The following is an outline that the students constructed prior to designing an interview guide.

An Ecological Look at African American Elderly
  1. A retrospective look at the African American elderly to increase understanding of their life courses and to learn what environmental factors influence their lives

     Education

     Geographic location (before and now)

     Changes over time: political involvement (participation) and impact on their lives

     Income—economics before and after

     Health issues

     Family relationships

     Religion

     Recreation and social activities

     Volunteer work

What it means to be Black, Negro, African American, or Colored (how they identify with the terms)

The Great Depression

The world wars

2. Research question/definition: What these persons' life experiences have been and how they have transacted with their environment to achieve and/or obtain

Goodness of fit

Adaptation

Nutrients

3. Assumptions

That life for the African American elderly has been difficult

That African American elderly have experienced racism

That African American elderly have experienced poverty

That nutrients from the wider environment were not readily available

That social networks played an important part in their lives

That religion played an important part in their lives

That African American elderly have developed unique coping strategies due to their experience

4. Demographics

Parents' background, birth places, and occupation

Same for self

Education

Spouses and children

5. Migration (if occurred) from South or other places (when, compelling reasons)

6. Satisfaction with lives now

7. If they had to do it over again, what they would do differently

8. What advice they would give a young Black person today on

AIDS

Teenage pregnancy

Gay/lesbian sexual orientations

South Africa

Russia

Sex

Marriage

Divorce

Interracial marriages

Drugs/alcohol

9. Best times in their lives

10. Worst times in their lives

In later semesters, the course was expanded from the African American experience to include other groups because "everybody has a story to tell." Student researchers were asked to select their own topics across all races and diverse issues. Following are some of the topics chosen by the students for their oral history research.

Student Projects
1. Oral histories of five people with severe physical disabilities living in the community: how people with severe disabilities adapt to living in the community and the needs for physical, social, psychological, and economic supports
2. A study of people more than 55 years old who volunteer in social service agencies and the needs they meet: how these people perceive the experience
3. The adaptation of the individual to major life transitions such as the transition to widowhood (for those over age 75)
4. Determinants important to adaptations of Black elderly to age-segregated congregate living
5. The adaptations of people with rheumatoid arthritis, including issues of environmental responses
6. Adoptees and birth parents: their search and reunion
7. Nursing home residents' perceptions of care and of the quality of life
8. Women known to a protective service agency who remain in abusive relationships: What external resources could be helpful?
9. Narratives from people living with AIDS and other life-threatening illnesses

The students conducted literature searches on these topics and wanted to hear the meanings of events in face-to-face interviews with the participants. Although the students' assumptions were sometimes validated, others found that their work generated new theories. They also became interested in social policy issues related to their respondents' lives, such as open adoption laws, the need for national health care coverage, and antidiscrimination and equal access to agencies for people with disabilities.

Other projects initiated at my suggestion were oral history interviews with recently arrived Russian Jewish émigrés, some of whom lived in the West Hartford community near the school, and an oral history research project in a nearby urban African American community (the Pliny Street Block Association). The purposes were (a) to empower the learners by teaching them the skills of oral history interviewing, (b) to allow them the opportunity to improve sensitivity to diverse populations, and (c) to help them learn about the adaptive capacities of the families. Full examples of these projects are presented in Chapters 7 and 10. A history of the local Urban League chapter was also done (Martin, 1993).

OTHER EFFORTS CONNECTING ORAL HISTORY AND SOCIAL WORK PRACTICE

Maluccio (1979), in *Learning From Clients,* reported a research project in which clients in a family service agency were interviewed in an oral history manner to determine their satisfaction (or lack of it) with the agency's services. Pratt (1987, 1989), a social worker, demonstrates in her oral history research how social service workers and educators worked with other disciplines and the community to learn about Blacks in Illinois. She, along with an English professor, student historians, and an anthropologist, collected oral histories, artifacts, and other documents, which they displayed at an exhibition. Members of the community were empowered as they became the teachers. They also became proud of their history as they better understood their adaptive strengths. The educators found a source of entry into the community as academia and the community together experienced the complex and interesting history of ordinary people.

This chapter described the theoretical perspectives I used in oral history research; examples of research in oral history by a variety of social work researchers, including seasoned practitioners, students, and community members; and the benefits to all involved. Oral history research in social work is based on the conviction that intellectual learning cannot replace direct relationship and exposure. In addition, if students must judge and assess, then they must attain the information on which to base judgments. The oral history method makes the experience of "outsiderness," its marginality, and its strengths available to all of us, thereby strengthening the knowledge base of the profession.

NOTE

1. From "Former Teacher Helped Mold Black Minds," by L. Hawes, *Tampa Tribune,* March 31, 1991, p. 6. Reprinted by permission.

REFERENCES

Billingsley, A. (1968). *Black families in White America.* Englewood Cliffs, NJ: Prentice Hall.

Blyden, E. W. (1908). *African life and customs.* London: C. M. Phillips.

Bruyn, S. T. (1966). *The human perspective in sociology: The methodology of participant observation.* Englewood Cliffs, NJ: Prentice Hall.

Chestang, L. (1979). Competence and knowledge in clinical social work: A dual perspective. In P. L. Ewalt (Ed.), *Towards a definition of clinical social work* (pp. 8-16). Washington, DC: National Association of Social Workers.

Draper, B. J. (1979). Black languages as an adaptive response to a hostile environment. In C. B. Germain (Ed.), *Social work practice, people and environment: An ecological perspective* (pp. 267-281). New York: Columbia University Press.

England, H. (1986). *Social work as art: Making sense for good practice.* London: Allen & Unwin.

Germain, C. B. (Ed.). (1979). *Social work practice, people and environment: An ecological perspective.* New York: Columbia University Press.

Germain, C. B., & Gitterman, A. (1980). *The life model of social work practice.* New York: Columbia University Press.

Glaser, B., & Strauss, A. (1967). *The discovery of grounded theory.* Chicago: Aldine.

Goldstein, H. (1990, January). The knowledge base of social work practice: Theory, wisdom, analogue, or art? *Families in Society: The Journal of Contemporary Human Services, 71*(1), 132-143.

Grinnell, R. M., Jr. (1981). *Social work research and evaluation.* Itasca, IL: F. E. Peacock.

Hawes, L. (1991, March 31). Former teacher helped mold Black minds. *Tampa Tribune,* p. 6.

Hill, R. (1972). *The strengths of Black families.* New York: Emerson-Hall.

Langer, L. L. (1991). *Holocaust testimonies: The ruins of memory.* New Haven, CT: Yale University Press.

Lewin, K. (1951). *Field theory in social science.* Westport, CT: Greenwood.

Logan, S. Freeman, E., & McRay, R. (1990). *Social work practice with Black families.* New York: Longman.

Maluccio, A. N. (1979). *Learning from clients: Interpersonal helping as viewed by clients and social workers.* New York: Free Press.

Martin, R. R. (1991, August). *Life forces of African American elderly illustrated through oral history narratives.* Paper presented at a conference on Qualitative Methods in Social Work Research Practice, State University of New York at Albany, School of Social Welfare, Nelson A. Rockefeller Institute of Government.

Martin, R. R. (1993). The first thirty years: An oral history of the Urban League. In S. Battle (Ed.), *The state of Black Hartford, Connecticut* (pp. 1-12). Hartford, CT: Urban League of Greater Hartford.

Martin, R. R. (1994). Life forces of African American elderly: Illustrated through oral history narratives. In E. Sherman & W. J. Reid (Eds.), *Qualitative research in social work* (pp. 190-199). New York: Columbia University Press.

Mbiti, J. S. (1970). *African religion and philosophy.* New York: Doubleday.

Norton, D. G. (1978). *The dual perspective: Inclusion of ethnic minority content in the social work curriculum.* New York: Council on Social Work Education.

Pratt, M. (Ed.). (1987). *We the people tell our story.* Bloomington, IL: Bloomington-Normal Black History Project.

Pratt, M. (Ed.). (1989). *Blacks in Illinois: The Bloomington-Normal experience: A program and exhibit.* Bloomington, IL: McLean County Museum.

Strauss, A. (1991, November). A personal history of the development of grounded theory. *Qualitative Family Research: A Newsletter of the Qualitative Family Research Network, 5*(5), 1-2.

3

MAKING A BRIDGE
Moving From Social Work Practice
Knowledge and Skill to Oral History Research Skill

After exploring the many uses in oral history, I hope I have piqued readers' interest enough that each might be asking, "Am I the right person to conduct the oral history research?" As Morrissey (1984) wrote,

> No oral historian can completely fit the job description with all its require-
> ments. Such a person would need to be a psychologist in order to master the
> art of building rapport, conducting interpersonal conversations about the
> past, and interpreting nonverbal communication; . . . a linguist in order to
> understand language and its meanings (especially if tapes are "translated"
> into transcripts); . . . know autobiography as a literary genre, and community
> and institutional studies as recommended by sociologists, . . . ethnographic
> studies conducted by anthropologists, . . . and the skills folk artists apply to
> myths, and intergenerational tradition. . . . [The oral historian] would need
> to wrestle intellectually with philosophical questions about truth and mean-
> ing. . . . He might wisely choose a course of study to include a "how to"
> interview. (p. xx)

Many social workers are by education and training competent to perform many of the tasks described. Following are some of the qualities that
I believe will help qualify the social work practitioner to conduct an oral
history. This is in no way intended to discount the seriousness and need
for good training and expertise in the art of oral history itself as described
by Morrissey.

When I look at social work education, this is what I see: Social workers are trained in the art of building rapport, conducting interpersonal conversations about the past, and interpreting nonverbal communication. In addition, social workers' interviewing skills are taught through course work and on-the-job training in field education. In social work education, students are exposed to the community and institutional contexts within which individual and group histories unfold. The importance of a liberal arts background (including biology) is stressed in the Council on Social Work Education's accreditation policies. The rules of "evidence" have long been taught in schools of social work, drawing on the pioneering work of Mary Richmond. In addition, although social workers are not linguists, we learn to "hear" the clients' language through their own interpretations.

RAPPORT

Social workers recognized early the importance of building rapport with clients. Drawing on Maeder's (1941) work, Biestik (1957) indicates that "rapport, a term borrowed from psychology, was quite popular with social workers for a long time" (p. 8). Biestik describes how the caseworker can effect rapport with the client. These are the same qualities practiced by the oral historian-interviewer. They include being "warm, natural, outgoing, at ease" (p. 8).

> The case worker [read also social worker and oral historian] will take steps to establish a relationship with the client as the so called emotional bridge over which factual data regarding the client and his problems will pass to the case worker [or oral historian], and back over which interpretations, enlightenments, and guidance will pass from case worker to client [interviewer to interviewee and vice versa]. (p. 8)

In addition to building rapport, social workers' methods of learning and practice draw on interviewing knowledge and skill to conduct interpersonal conversation about the past and interpret nonverbal communication.

Hepworth and Larsen (1986) write that the process of engaging clients successfully (or engaging participants in a research project) involves trust in the practitioner's helpful, honest intent. A condition of rapport is that participants perceive the practitioner as understanding and as genuinely interested in their well-being, in learning about them as individuals, and in learning about their culture. For example, one of my student researchers volunteered to teach English to Southeast Asian immigrants. She related that one of the highlights of her research was when the interviewees said to her, "Thank you for being interested in our culture" (*Vietnam, Cambodia, and Laos,* 1992, p. 2).

Oral historians often manifest the same values and attitudes of the profession of social work. These include (a) nonjudgmental attitudes, (b) acceptance, (c) clients' rights of self-determination, and (d) respect for clients' worth and dignity, uniqueness and individuality, and problem-solving capacities (Hepworth & Larsen, 1986). Gwaltney (1980) believes in an additional requirement for conducting oral history in the African American community and, by inference, with other oppressed minorities. He writes that the researcher must have "a proper regard for security and reciprocity . . . [which is] . . . vital to the establishment of rapport in core Black enclaves. The prudent are wary and slow to bestow confidence" (p. xxiv). Oral histories provide for researchers an avenue into the African American community that might otherwise be cordoned off because of wariness on the part of prudent African Americans. Social workers, through empathy and social work interview technique, must be sensitive to the adaptive wariness of minority group members.

Green (1982) states,

> It is commonplace in much of social work, especially in those areas involving direct encounters with clients, that the successful worker must establish rapport and develop empathic relationships in order to further treatment objectives. . . . One assumption though rarely stated . . . is that the designated "helping skills" (i.e., empathy, warmth, and genuineness, student's enhanced perception of verbal and nonverbal cues, attention to emotional states during interaction, and styles of questioning and responding) are uniformly applicable to most, if not all clients, and to most client problems; that the worker need only refine these skills in order to develop the warm, trusting relationship that is the mark of the professional in working with others. (pp. 50-51)

Like Green, I argue that such techniques as described above are not in and of themselves a sufficient basis for working with minority clients. For example, in Chapter 6, I state that the Black community is slow to bestow trust and explained how I found in my own research that they wanted to know me as a person and seemed to judge my qualifications on the basis of where I came from, what church I attended, where I went to college, what sorority I was a member of, if I had children, and where they were.

All these questions were asked to allow them to somehow determine my genuineness and to understand if I was ethnic (African American) and competent enough to hear and understand their stories. Although I am

African American, I still had to pass the tests. Non-African Americans might be asked some different questions, but the intent is the same: "Can you hear what I am saying and appreciate who I am?" Puerto Rican and other Latino clients also expect *personalismo* of their social workers or interviewers (Garcia-Preto, 1982).

Ethnic competence, then, does not propose that trained individuals are those who can mimic the behavioral routines and linguistic particularities of their minority clients. Nor does it rule that out. Its emphasis is on the trained worker's ability to adapt professional tasks and work styles to the cultural values and preferences of clients.

HOW TO INTERVIEW

As Garrett (1942) points out,

For an interview to be successful, the diverse fears of both interviewer and interviewee must be allayed, and the diverse desires of both must be met. Rapport must be established by the two, a relationship that will enable the interviewee to reveal the essential facts of his situation and that will enable the interviewer to be most effective in helping him. (p. 9)

One group, who are interviewers par excellence, are social caseworkers. Their tasks make them professional interviewers, and for some of them interviewing becomes an art and indeed, almost a science, some of whose basic principles at least they are able to formulate and organize into the beginnings of a systematic body of knowledge. (p. 7)

Reynolds (1985) wrote,

The art, or skill, of professional social work consists of activities which cannot be standardized. One can no more train a person to be a good interviewer than to write good poems. One has to bring to bear what ability he has to see and hear and feel, and to perceive the meaning of what is before him. (pp. 52-53)

The interviewer must, therefore, have self-awareness and understanding to enter into the situation of the client without disrupting what is there but enhancing the "ability of the people who live in it to play their part" (Reynolds, 1985, p. 53). Practitioners must give of themselves and take only what is required in mutual interchange of ideas and feeling, so that the solving of the problem may be a cooperative one. Reynolds insists that workers must be educated, not trained to technique alone, which means being educated as whole persons. The acquisition of an art is not quickly learned. It is a lifelong and growing achievement.

Garrett (1942) describes eight techniques that social workers use well and that oral historians might well use to guide them in the interview process. The eight techniques are (a) observation, (b) listening, (c) beginning where the client is, (d) questioning, (e) talking, (f) answering personal questions, (g) leadership or direction, and (h) interpretation. A danger, however, exists in that a person may seize on certain of the techniques that are highly valuable in certain cases and with certain populations and apply them arbitrarily without consideration of who the client is.

COMMUNICATION

Nonverbal communication is "listening with the eyes as well as the ears," listening "to the silent language of gestures as well as to the spoken language of voice" (Kadushin, 1990, p. 269). Kadushin spells out a variety of sources of significant nonverbal data: chronomics, smell, touch, artifactual communication, paralinguistics, proxemics, and body language-kinesics.

Chronomics refers to time as a general nonverbal message. Everyone has heard jokes about clients who arrive late, early, or on time. We practitioners sometimes keep the participant waiting. I inform researchers, however, that oral history does not allow us the opportunity to flatter ourselves. Now that we are the seekers of information, we can only hope the participants are generous with their time.

"Smell, the olfactory channel, a source of considerable communication for lower animals," says Kadushin (1990), "is rarely, if ever, investigated or discussed as a useful source of human communication." Further, he says, "We make judgements about families based on the smells we smell as we come into a house on a home visit" (p. 271).

Touch, which Kadushin (1990) describes as "tactile sensory communications" (p. 271), is rarely used in interviews. The custom of touching, however, varies among different ethnic groups. Artifactual communication is the language of objects. "The channel is the visual channel and the source of communication is the physical setting and personal adornments—clothes, hairstyles, makeup, jewelry, etc." (p. 275). The house visits provide that open window to the world of the oral history participant. Paralinguistics is "the auditory channel, the transmission and reception of 'noises' the participants make" (p. 279). Researchers or practitioners will often read transcripts of the tapes. Oral history tapes, however, are a rich source of material as researchers listen to the tone, pitch, and age of a voice, and so forth. "Proxemics is the language of space and difference" (p. 281). This invisible boundary is different for different cultures. I give an example of this when I discuss how a Puerto Rican student demonstrated to the class her culture's acceptance of a close-up conversation (see Chapter 4).

Body language-kinesics, which concerns movements, gestures, and posture, is an important form of nonverbal communication. Kadushin (1990) shares such movements as jumping for joy and covering eyes when ashamed; posture and whole body communication, such as sitting erect or slouched; facial expressions of many different types, including the eyes; and gestures: The hands and arms, feet and legs are all forms of communication that help to regulate conversation.

The oral historian can learn much from silent language when interviewing a participant from a different culture. First, the participant may remain silent or respond slowly because this is his or her cultural norm. Or a participant may be attempting to retrieve information from the past. It might also mean that the researcher has approached a topic that the interviewee prefers not to discuss. In a face-to-face interview, the researcher-practitioner noticing this hesitation or body language might say to the respondent, "It appears that this discussion makes you uncomfortable." It may also present the opportunity for the oral historian to ask for further clarification of an issue.

LINGUISTICS

Although not trained in linguistics, social workers, by their commitment to studying human diversity, are trained to take into consideration other cultures and social classes and their language and meanings. Social workers and oral historians are taught to "check it out" when not clear as to the meaning of words or phrases. For example, if an interviewee says, "I punished my child," the interviewer might want to clarify if this was physical punishment or if the child's punishment was not being allowed to watch a favorite television program. A knowledge of the client's cultural milieu is necessary in understanding the client as well as in understanding the meaning of the language. It is important to view the culture up close through the cultural lens of the participant.

Although few social workers can boast expertise in linguistics, social workers tend to have the participants interpret the meaning of their language in dialogue. Solomon (1986), in her chapter on direct social work practice with African Americans, suggests that African Americans may have a tendency to communicate ideas and feelings by analogy rather than by analysis.

A good understanding of languages is extremely important. This became apparent to me after I presented a tape of oral history research of Black southern elders transcribed by a young White woman from the midwestern states to an audience of African American professionals. I distributed copies of the transcribed tape and asked the audience to follow along as I played the original cassette tape. By the time we were into the second paragraph, I noted the professionals making corrections on the transcribed sheets. Soon they began to reveal discomfort in their body language. I stopped the tape and asked for feedback. "Did a White person transcribe this tape?" I was asked. To my response, Why do you ask?, I was told that it was plain that this transcriber did not understand Black language. "We are hearing clearly from that tape, this man did not say what is typed here." Some of his statements were changed to reflect the typist's own language and biases. For example, the participant was explaining about the changes in mass society: "When you were a youth, you couldn't go out on a basketball court and stay until ten o'clock. The city wouldn't let the lights stay on. But now in order to keep them out of devilment . . ." Instead of the latter phrase, however, the transcriber wrote, "out of the element." The participant also spoke of parent and teacher relationships and the changes that have occurred: "Now they go and fuss the teacher down." The transcriber wrote, "bash the teacher down." In another case, the transcriber wrote "patent themselves after" instead of "pattern themselves after." These examples of language changes may not appear excessive. When I explain, however, that these four changes and others not listed are found in only two pages of narratives, one might better understand the Black audience's reaction. This exchange was followed by a discussion about the need in the profession and in the public school system for the understanding of Black language. We cannot know how much young Black children are penalized in school because of teachers' failure to understand Black language, nor can we imagine what disservice a client might endure by the failure of Whites to clearly understand the language. The oral history methodology is one excellent way to address such issues.

COMMUNITY AND INSTITUTIONAL STUDIES

Rivera and Erlich (1992), in *Community Organizing in a Diverse Society,* provide a summary of 12 qualities that they believe contribute to the success of a community organizer. One of the 12 that students have used in conducting oral history research has been to gather "knowledge of past strategies, their strengths, and limitations" (p. 15). Rivera and Erlich argue,

> It is critical that organizers (managers, supervisors of staff, community developers and others engaged in macro practice, as well) develop and share an historical knowledge base that helps identify the many mistakes made to finally illuminate those techniques that appeared to have recently worked best in similar situations. (p. 15)

In *The Community and the Social Worker,* Fellin (1995) stresses the need for social workers to probe and understand the multiple communities (communities of identification and interest beyond the immediate neighborhood) to which their clients belong. In Chapters 8 and 10 of this book, I give examples of how oral histories can be used to work with community groups.

LIBERAL ARTS CURRICULUM

The Council on Social Work Education, the accrediting body for the social work curriculum, requires certain liberal arts prerequisites for admission to schools of social work. Among these are courses such as history, economics, biology, political science, and psychology. This broad-based liberal arts education provides excellent background for the oral historian.

Social workers have the unique training, characteristics, knowledge, skill, and educational backgrounds that make them the logical heirs to the title "oral historian." Social workers are ready to claim this heritage and use our collective knowledge to embrace the oral history methodology.

USES OF ORAL HISTORY IN
INTERPERSONAL DIRECT PRACTICE

In earlier writing (Martin, 1987), I outlined and described the usefulness of oral history throughout the social work curriculum. I made suggestions for incorporating oral histories into the major curriculum areas, which are practice methods courses, field practicum, human behavior courses, social welfare policy courses, and research courses. Here I focus on the uses of oral history in direct practice.

Hartman (1990) argues that "it is a difficult time to be a social work practitioner," although "it has never been easy" (p. 44). She describes the turmoil that has encompassed modern society, including a number of complex and devastating problems and challenges,

> many of which we are well familiar such as the AIDS and drug epidemic, add to that the upward spiraling of tuberculosis, and the demands for both differentiation and cohesion in an increasingly diverse society, widespread family and street violence, hopelessness, stress resulting from changing gender roles, adolescent suicide, the public's refusal to acknowledge sexual preference orientations and abortion rights. (p. 44)

In addition, the spiraling of the country's economic debt and job loss is systematically excluding millions of people, many of whom are young people of color, from the opportunity structure. In Chapter 6 of this book on Black adaptation, the narrator reflects mass society changes in his discussion of Black youth, concluding "but the average [Black] kid doesn't have a chance." Oral history makes the interviewee the expert and teacher and the practitioner the learner. This is a practice stance that helps empower clients in direct social work practice (Lee, 1994). The subsequent chapters in Part II of this book give the reader a chance to learn directly from the interviewee's own words even as they must learn to value the client's "different voice" (Gilligan, 1984).

IMPLICATIONS FOR
SOCIAL WORK EDUCATION

Hartman (1990) notes, "It is also a difficult time to be a social work educator, challenged to prepare students to join the ranks of professional social workers in attempting to help individuals and families, to devise creative programs, to work for social change" (p. 44)—and, I might add, to understand the subjective reality of individuals and families who have been left out by the system. "The profession," Hartman asserts, "must draw together. Education and practitioners need to collaborate, share their expertise, and support each other in the achievement of the profession's mission" (p. 44). I am arguing that one way to accomplish this might be to use the method of oral history research to build new knowledge, to enhance integration of professional and humanistic values, and to open up new concepts and interpretations of a subject.

The following are potential practice and educational objectives that might be achieved through use of oral histories:

- Understanding of the participants' meanings
- Cognitive and affective understanding of and sensitivity and appreciation for minority and other oppressed people's experiences
- Firsthand knowledge of the history of minorities, women, and other subgroups in America
- Increased understanding of societal conflict; political, organizational, cultural, social, and economic forces; and the effects of oppression on people's needs, rights, and aspirations
- Increased awareness of individual biases and heightened professionalism and sensitivity in working with minority individuals and families
- Broader knowledge of linkages and resources in minority, female, and oppressed communities, including their nutritive qualities
- Knowledge and understanding of the values, strengths, and resiliency of minority and other subgroup families
- Increased knowledge of assessment and interventive strategies with minorities of color, women, and other oppressed groups from the point of view of people who might well be seen as clients at another time

Practitioners learn (a) to supplement material on less known subjects, (b) to communicate across social and racial barriers, and (c) to gain understanding of the reciprocal influences of minority families and their social environment within the context of a racist or oppressive society. Oral historians can also provide a vehicle for students to learn how to begin where the client is and to tune in to the participant's sense of life forces and urgency. The very processes of listening can facilitate client empowerment by giving the client the respect that is a sine qua non of taking responsibility. This was made clear by a narrator's quote of the statement made to a protective service worker: "Just listen" (Boyle-Glidden, Cummings, & Dryjowicz-Burek, 1992, p. 14). In addition, oral history can aid students in assessing the many realities and meanings (i.e., theirs, the participants', the community's, and the agency's funding sources) and the need to make assessment on the basis of these realities.

I have found the following techniques useful in introducing learners and others to the oral history approach:

1. Review videotapes of oral history interviews. Ask,
   What are consistent themes?
   Are there examples of adversity?

What coping techniques are observed or stated?

What meaning does the participant give to events?

2. Listen to tapes of an oral history interview. Analyze the tapes and study the interviewing techniques.

3. Typical issues to explore include the networking used by interviewee and how the interviewee defines his or her resource systems. Ask questions such as these:

What power blockages are mentioned?

What does the taped conversation tell about the culture of the participant and about the history of his or her people?

What difficulty, if any, do you have in following the conversation?

What do the voice and tone tell about the participant?

4. Help learners also focus on themselves. Ask,

What biases did you become aware of?

Are these your own or those of the informant?

THE PRACTICUM

Oral histories are a rich source of experiential and didactic learning in the student practicum. They are also useful in helping experienced practitioners gain advanced understanding of a client population. The field practicum provides students with opportunities to reconcile the artificial practice-research split. They now have the forum to integrate and practice both interviewing and engagement skills and research methodology. Supervisors and field practicum instructors might find oral history methodology useful to help learners and practitioners (a) discuss their experiences as they venture into minority communities; (b) learn about clients who are different from the worker; (c) explore personal biases, feelings, and thoughts as they begin to work in minority communities; and (d) compare different neighborhoods and lifestyles.

Clearly, knowledge of the oral history method enriches social work practice and education on all levels, and social work education, in turn, makes a bridge to oral history research as well. I turn now to the "how-to" of oral history research.

REFERENCES

Biestik, F. P. (1957). *The casework relationship.* Chicago: Loyola University Press.

Boyle-Glidden, S., Cummings, B., & Dryjowicz-Burek, N. (1992, April). *Domestic violence: Women's perspectives: An oral history research project.* Student research project, University of Connecticut, School of Social Work, West Hartford.

Fellin, P. (1995). *The community and the social worker* (2nd ed.). Itasca, IL: F. E. Peacock.

Garcia-Preto, N. (1982). Puerto Rican families. In M. McGoldrick, J. K. Pearce, & J. Giordana (Eds.), *Ethnicity and family therapy* (pp. 164-186). New York: Guilford.

Garrett, A. (1942). *Interviewing: Its principles and methods.* New York: Family Service Association of America.

Gilligan, C. (1984). *In a different voice: Psychological theory and women's development.* Cambridge, MA: Harvard University Press.

Green, J. W. (1982). *Cultural awareness in the human services.* Englewood Cliffs, NJ: Prentice Hall.

Gwaltney, J. C. (1980). *Drylongso: A self-portrait of Black America.* New York: Random House.

Hartman, A. (1990). Education for direct practice. *Families in Society: The Journal of Contemporary Human Services, 71*(1), 44-50.

Hepworth, D. H., & Larsen, J. A. (1986). *Direct social work practice: Theory and skills* (2nd ed.). Chicago: Dorsey.

Kadushin, A. (1990). *The social work interview* (3rd ed.). New York: Columbia University Press.

Lee, J. A. B. (1994). *The empowerment approach to social work practice.* New York: Columbia University Press.

Maeder, L. M. A. (1941, October). Diagnostic criteria: The concept of normal and abnormal. *The Family, 22*(6), 171-179.

Martin, R. R. (1987). Oral history in social work education: Chronicling the Black experience. *Journal of Social Work Education, 23*(3), 5-10.

Morrissey, C. (1984). Introduction. In D. K. Dunaway & W. K. Baum (Eds.), *Oral history: An interdisciplinary anthology* (pp. xix-xxiii). Nashville, TN: American Association for State and Local History.

Reynolds, B. C. (1985). *Learning and teaching in social work.* Silver Springs, MD: National Association of Social Workers.

Rivera, F. G., & Erlich, J. L. (Eds.). (1992). *Community organizing in a diverse society.* Needham Heights, MA: Allyn & Bacon.

Solomon, B. B. (1986). Social work with Afro-Americans. In A. Morales & B. Sheafor (Eds.), *Social work: A profession of many faces* (pp. 416-436). Needham Heights, MA: Allyn & Bacon.

Vietnam, Cambodia, and Laos: An oral history analysis of the Southeast Asian refugee experience. (1992, February). Student research project, University of Connecticut, School of Social Work, West Hartford.

4

GENERATING AND RECORDING ORAL HISTORIES
Process and Method

BEGINNING THE RESEARCH
PROCESS: FINDING THE QUESTION

In this chapter, I discuss the process and method of oral history research. The oral history process begins, as does all research, with the inquisitive mind, curiosity or concern, and the desire to ask questions. In my experience, beginning researchers are often anxious and are likely to have many questions about the process. Among the questions are these: How do we select a topic or an issue? How do we learn what information already exists? How do we know what information we need? Who among these "wisdom keepers" are willing to tell the story? How do we select participants? Where will we find participants?

I attempt to reassure new researchers by explaining that the list of topics can be as varied as there are people: What are they interested in? A particular era of history? Or do they want to know about special groups such as the elderly or ethnic minorities? About gender or sexual orientation issues in general or something specific such as survivors of the Great Depression?

I share examples of research projects. One example students particularly like is that of a student researcher who recently interviewed elderly women living in the Greater Hartford area who were in their late teens or early 20s during the Depression. To engage them, she took their pictures and gave them copies of their pictures as they remembered their lives. They were eager to share how women viewed their world during that era.

THE STEPS IN THE PROCESS

1. Selection of topic or issue (the project)
2. Literature review (Select key terms and words from stated topic or research questions. Use these key terms and words to do a library search. Caution: Be careful before concluding that nothing exists on the topic.)
3. Definition of the selected topic or issues
4. Formulation of tentative assumption (What research question(s) is the researcher trying to answer?)
5. Statement of the research purpose in action verbs (e.g., "The purpose of this study is to explore . . ." or "to describe . . .")
6. Systematic identification of the participants and the site/setting
7. Interviews and data collection (on the road!)
8. Transcribing
9. Editing
10. Analyzing and interpreting the data (involves logical analysis, *not* statistical analysis)
11. Writing up the project

Kathleen Emerson, a student who took my oral history research class in the spring semester of 1993, has consented for me to share her thorough research project. I use examples of her research, along with examples of my own research, throughout this chapter (and also in Chapter 5) to show the process and method.

SELECTING THE PROJECT

Selection of the project is Step 1 in the process. First, the researcher needs to consider the amount of time available to conduct the research because this helps determine the size of the sample, the scope of the area to be investigated, and whether to transcribe tapes. Emerson chose to conduct her research with women who have had breast cancer. She chose this topic because of (a) her interest in learning about women's coping responses to breast cancer, (b) an interest in the "making of meaning" (symbolic interactionism), and (c) her personal concerns and fears. A woman is at risk of developing breast cancer simply because of gender. It has been estimated that one out of nine women will have the disease at some time during her life.

LITERATURE REVIEW

Step 2 in the research process is the literature review. In oral history, this can be conducted before, during, or after the research. Saying it is a "second step" is somewhat arbitrary. There are pluses and minuses for the findings regardless of the timing of the literature search. I have learned that it is useful to have background information before starting the field research. On the other hand, I sometimes find that to have some information in advance causes me to close my mind to new information that the participant shares. One of my student practitioners conducted a literature search, started his interviewing, and realized that his search had suggested only a few important determinants to high levels of satisfaction for Black elders in age-segregated housing. In his first few interviews, his interviewees discussed self-determination and family supports as determinants. The student then did further research on these determinants, which he found discussed in other periodicals. He then used deductive logic, that of fitting the theory to the research instead of moving with a fixed agenda.

Emerson began her research by reading about women and breast cancer. She also read Gilligan's (1984) *In a Different Voice* to better understand women's development of self in relation to others. As the research progressed, she searched other literature as needed for further knowledge and clarification of issues.

DEFINING THE SELECTED TOPIC OR ISSUES

Step 3 is to define the selected issues. In this step, the general topic is broken down into manageable questions, and the researcher selects one or more researchable questions. Once a topic is selected, the researcher must operationalize the major concepts.

In a grounded theory approach (see Chapter 2), Emerson (1993) chose to visit one woman who had experienced a mastectomy to experience the interview process and to learn some of the subjective issues so that she might intelligently approach other participants (see Glaser & Strauss, 1967). Emerson relates,

I developed a series of about 25 relatively open-ended questions related to the above areas of interest and concern. I felt that there might be a strong likelihood that I would want to revise some of these questions after I began and thought that this might be a likelihood because I always assume that the template of my own concerns might not necessarily fit with the real concerns and interests of those going through an experience. I wanted to be sure that this was not a restrictive or artificial overlay to the real concerns of the people I interviewed. I therefore decided that I would do a "pre-interview" interview with an articulate, thoughtful woman in my agency. I would both "test" my questions and areas of concern, and ask for suggestions as to gaps, better ways to work items in order to "get at" what I wanted to get at, sequence of questions, and so forth. I asked fairly specific questions at the end of the interview (off tape) regarding the interview itself and related to the areas just mentioned. This was very helpful. The feedback helped me to feel positive about my interview skills and the specific advice about areas and concerns to add and highlight were invaluable in modifying the interview.

An area that I had not stressed was that of the role of spirituality in recovery, perceptions of strength, and health; and differences in the role of spirituality in one's life before and after learning of the breast cancer. Another area that I had not thought to specifically highlight but that became evident in the pre-interview was that of learning to be "selfish" and "caring for one's self" and not "feeling guilty about it." It also helped me to think about the possible role of time (that is, how long had the respondent been dealing with the disease?) on types of strategies employed for self-care, gathering information, and feeling of vulnerability and helplessness. In general, I felt that the decision to do this "pre-interview" was a good one. In addition, this respondent was able to give me some good ideas as to where to go for other participants to give me credibility with several support and therapy groups. I called the various group leaders and asked them if they would mention my study and interview and find out if I might contact members to discuss it and possibly set up an interview. (pp. 2-3)

From this first interview, Emerson generated categories to explore and developed a number of open-ended questions (listed below), which she hoped to cover during the project.

Sample Interview Questions
1. How did you find out that you had breast cancer?
2. What were your thoughts and feelings when you found out you had breast cancer? Can you remember what it felt like at the time?
3. What were the first steps that you took in confronting (dealing with) the disease?
4. How did you decide on treatment for your breast cancer? How involved do you feel you were in making these decisions? How would you describe

your interactions/relationships with the medical establishment? What aspects did you find most satisfactory/unsatisfactory? What stood out most for you about these interactions? How would you characterize these interactions?

5. Where did you get support during this experience, and how did you go about getting it? How did you involve your family in this? Who else did you involve? What or who was the greatest source of support and strength for you during this experience?

6. Were there pulls between your own needs and your family's needs?

7. Has the length of time coping with the disease changed the way you cope with it? If so, how?

8. Do you have any theories or beliefs about what may have caused this disease?

9. What is the role of spirituality in your life before and after receiving your diagnosis?

10. Have your feelings about yourself and life gone through any changes from when you first learned that you had breast cancer? If so, could you please describe their progress and changes?

11. What was the hardest thing for you about your experience?

12. What have you learned from this experience?

13. In retrospect, do you think that you would have done anything differently regarding your experience?

14. If you were going to talk to (give advice to) other women about breast cancer, what would you tell them? (Emerson, 1993, p. 5)

FORMULATING TENTATIVE ASSUMPTIONS

Step 4 is to formulate tentative assumptions. In quantitative research, a hypothesis often describes or suggests a relationship between two or more variables that is subject to empirical test. In other words, it is a statement of specific expectations about the nature of things that the researcher wishes to test to confirm or deny hunches or theoretical expectations by real data. This is not so in oral history research. Qualitative research does not begin with a hypothesis; nevertheless, to enter the field without having given some thought as to expectations is foolhardy.

Oral history studies may begin as grounded theory does, with vaguely formulated research questions that interviewees' experiences will refine, leading to new questions (Glaser & Strauss, 1967; Martin, 1987, 1988, 1991; Taylor & Bogdan, 1984). Glaser and Strauss (1967) developed grounded theory, a term used in reference to the creation of theory that is based on observation more than deduction. Babbie (1983) describes the two logical methods, deduction and induction, that link social science theory and research. Deduction involves the derivation of expectations or hypotheses from theories. Induction involves the development of generalizations from specific observations. Taylor and Bogdan (1984) describe the process of grounded theory as building theory from the bottom up—that is, being open to what the site has to offer rather than attempting to make data fit the theory.

Van Maanen (1983) suggests that "to theorize well in advance of our facts" allows for the "possibility that the facts that emerge from our studies are twisted to fit a given theory" (p. 37). Miles (1983) notes that "the need to develop grounded theory usually exists in tension with the need for clarity and focus" (p. 119). This means not beginning a research project without some assumptions. I suggest that researchers develop a framework for beginning the research and revise it as the project progresses.

Emerson's assumptions about the outcome of her work were that she would find the women

trying to make sense of experience (giving it meaning);

having more fear, more sense of loss, less sense of control, and less optimism and hope; and

experiencing women's political/personal issues of control, boundaries, struggles with a distinct sense of self, and the effect on relationships and efforts at sorting these out.

STATING THE RESEARCH PURPOSE

Step 5 in the oral history process is stated in action verbs. For example, the purpose of this research is to learn about selected women's experiences with breast cancer, to ask a series of questions while listening attentively to the women's responses to help the women reveal their stories, and to learn how women cope with breast cancer.

SYSTEMATIC IDENTIFICATION
OF THE PARTICIPANTS

Step 6 begins with sampling of the participants and identifying the site and setting. One method of sampling that I have used in conducting oral history projects is the snowball technique (Atherton & Klemmack, 1982).

This method allows the researcher to select an interviewee who identifies the next interviewee. This is also an excellent technique when the community is wary of the researcher and of the researcher's intentions. Another technique is to start with a small number of persons to be interviewed who have knowledge of the topic being researched and have them specify others who have knowledge of the topic. For example, in my study of Black family adaptation, families selected to participate in the study were identified and first contacted by the Urban League of Greater Tampa and the Family Services Association of Tampa. Members of three of the oldest (more than 100 years old) Black churches in the area and peers also identified families. Fifteen families were selected according to the participants' community of residence, birthplace, and century and decade of birth. Each participant must have been living in the community for 50 years prior to the undertaking of the study. An example of this project is found in Chapter 6.

In the oral history research method, the investigator's sources of information are known as primary and secondary sources. *Primary* sources of data are individuals with firsthand knowledge of the event(s) being investigated. These sources are eyewitness reports of the occurrences. In Emerson's research, she interviewed primary sources. Those who only heard about an event at that time or who received accounts secondhand are *secondary* sources. When conducting oral history research, I try to be clear about the sources of the data interviewees call on. For example, regarding the Great Depression, did the interviewees witness the era, did someone tell them about that period, or did they read an account of that time?

A question frequently asked is how I or other oral historians can know whether we have been told the truth, and does this matter? The question rephrased is whether this type of research meets the test of external and internal validity. I will define these two concepts in the context of oral history. *Reliability* is defined as the consistency with which an individual will tell the same story about the same event on a number of different occasions. *Validity* defines the degree of conformity between the reports of the event and the event itself, as recorded by other primary resource materials such as photographs, family Bibles, diaries, school reports, letters, and other documents. A participant may give a report that is true, however, the test of validity is that the report be measured against another body of evidence. I have found such evidence to support much of my research. Nevertheless, researchers cannot forget that some "evidence" regarding the history of oppressed groups such as African Americans may be half-truths or untruths or may have no "objective" truths available. The best truth may be the oral history because it gives the subjective truth of life's events.

I consider an oral history informant to be reliable if his or her report of events are consistent. In my research, I have been impressed when participants-informants describe the same events, often supporting their stories with documents. This was especially true in the case of people who shared information about their struggle for equalization of salary, which was described in Chapter 2.

There will be times when an informant does not tell the story the same way each time. I advise researchers to question the informant about the inconsistency before they decide the informant is not telling the truth. The interviewee may give a logical explanation for the inconsistency. The oral historian gets an opportunity to question the informant. There is also a level of subjective truth about life events that transcends the absolute facts of a situation. This is the level of veracity oral historians seek most.

How to Select Participants

1. The participant should be able to speak with authority about what the researcher is investigating. This person may be illiterate and uneducated as well as literate and educated.
2. The interviewee could have been in an influential or noninfluential position at the time of the event or might have viewed the event as an outsider. The researcher is more interested in what people are available to tell the stories about events and give meaning to the stories than in social standing or absolute firsthand experience.
3. The participant might be an old-timer who can tell about the past; a representative member of a group; or an associate of a particular person, period, or event.
4. The search should be diversified. Researchers may want to avoid selecting and interviewing only participants of the same social class or persons with similar perceptions or beliefs about a topic that affects many people in one community. Homogeneity can generate bias. People will often present the subjective reality about issues. Therefore, as much as possible, researchers should try to hear all sides of an issue.

NOTE OF CAUTION

Once the investigator has chosen a research topic and learned who the keepers of the information are, it is important to begin research right away. Often several prospective participants may move, die, or become incapacitated. I became painfully aware of this possibility quite recently when I was conducting an oral history project of families of ex-slaves who had fled to Canada. I interviewed one participant in August, intending to return the following August to edit the transcribed tape and to clarify additional data, only to learn in May of that following year prior to my second trip that the participant had died of complications arising in surgery.

Another participant whom I had come to know during my previous trip in August and had hoped to interview on this second trip also died. I found myself at his graveside while his family mourned his death. In fact, six of the participants died during this 3-year span. These examples should make researchers more cognizant that life may intervene and that a study should be as quick and focused as possible.

INTERVIEWS AND DATA COLLECTION

In Step 7 in the oral history research process, data are collected according to the oral history methodology. The researcher has already determined the method for collecting data, including assumptions; sampling—who, where, and why; and open-ended interviews. In beginning the interviews and data collection, the researcher should be open to what the site has to offer and keep in mind that research has a purpose. To accomplish the purpose, the researcher will have participants tell their stories and listen for the meanings expressed.

LEARNING FROM PARTICIPANTS: CULTURAL COMPETENCE

An important sign of respect, particularly in the African American community, is "putting a handle on people's names," an old Black folks' way of saying to call people "Miss," "Mrs.," "Dr.," and the like. This shows proper regard and proper respect for persons who because of race or color may have suffered more than their share of indignities.

I became especially cognizant of this once when I took my class into the African American community, using the Urban League office as our base. The director and staff heard the students referring to me by my first name. When the class took a break, they expressed to me their concern with such behavior. From their perspectives, the students had crossed the boundaries of good manners. This was more apparent because several Black elderly persons, who spoke to the class, referred to me as "Professor" or "Dr. Martin." It is important to learn what the culture expects or dictates. Green (1982) refers to this as "ethnic competence." The definition, he writes, "implies an awareness of prescribed and proscribed behavior within a specific culture, and it suggests that the ethnically-competent worker has the ability to carry out professional activities consistent with this awareness" (p. 52). One way researchers can ensure that they are being culturally astute is to ask the participants what they wish to be called.

In one of my classes, students learned about the Puerto Rican culture and the person's sense of space. The class participated in a demonstration of "individual space." One Puerto Rican social worker stood close up face-to-face with another Puerto Rican, and they began to verbally communicate with each other. No degree of discomfort was noted. She then stood face-to-face with a non-Puerto Rican member from the class. The student began to experience a sense of discomfort, which she demonstrated by backing away slightly. The class was able to visualize and discuss the differences in cultural orientation. The Puerto Rican worker also explained that non-Puerto Rican social workers entering Puerto Rican homes may tend to see the homes as chaotic, with many people talking at once. In actuality, family members communicate well and selectively particularize the conversations in the room. Of course, there are variations within and between subgroups of a culture.

Cuban social workers in this class talked about the need to distinguish between the Cuban immigrants who came before Castro's rise and those who came after and between White and Black Cubans. Class members also visited neighborhood clubs: Italian, Spanish, and Cuban, both Black and White. Students learned about these cultures, how the Spanish and Cuban communities were separated from the White and African American communities, and how they built their own enclaves.

LETTERS OF INTRODUCTION

Another important consideration in the process of preparing for interviews is what I consider safety for the interviewer and the interviewee. With all the violence in the communities, elderly participants may fear letting people into their homes without some form of identification. Other participants may also be leery. In addition, the interviewer may have heard many rumors or have myths about the lack of safety in minority communities. I have, therefore, devised a letter of introduction written on university letterhead, to be used by the learners as an identification card and to request the participants' help. If an agency director or community center director has assisted in identifying participants, a letter is also sent requesting the director to assist the researchers.

DATA COLLECTION AND
DATA-GATHERING INSTRUMENTS

Open-ended questions allow the interviewer to be open to what the site has to offer, to develop theory from the bottom up, and to secure information that will provide insight into the respondent's reality and give meaning to his or her life space through time. I have found it helpful to use an ecological map—an "eco-map" (Hartman, 1978, p. 469). This is a diagrammatic assessment of family and other relationships, a simple pencil-and-paper simulation that maps the ecological system. In the center of a piece of paper, I draw a square or rectangle (it could also be a circle, with heavy lines). Within that square, I write the family names, nuclear and extended. In recognition of the many changes in definition of the family, I write *marriage, divorced, single parent, adopted kin, gay/lesbian, blended families,* and the like. The heavy lines around this square are used to represent the boundaries of the family. I also see the lines as a representation of the participants' "castle." One enters into this world for research purposes by "invitation." (See the ecological map shown in Figure 4.1.)

Once I describe the relevant family constellation, I consider other variables that might apply. I might have uncovered them through research or from having experienced the culture. In my project on Black families, I drew circles on the paper and inserted *housing, economic indicators, friends and neighbors, education, religion,* and so forth. As my research progressed, I added new circles. Other times, I have begun with just a few simple questions in mind and have built on them as the interview shifts its focus on the basis of new information.

USING THE TAPE
RECORDER FOR DATA COLLECTION

A tape recorder allows interviewers to capture much more than they could by relying on memory. The interview data consist almost entirely of words. Unlike participant observers, interviewers do not have the leisure of unobtrusive observation, but they do have to "capture the words." Many of the most important life histories in the social sciences would never have been written without the use of electronic recording devices (Taylor & Bogdan, 1984). In his introduction to the *Children of Sanchez,* Lewis (1963) writes, "The tape recorder, used in taking down the life histories in this book, has made possible the beginning of a new kind of literature of social realism" (p. 11).

Before actually beginning to collect data by using the tape recorder, researchers should become familiar with some specific guidelines. Stave

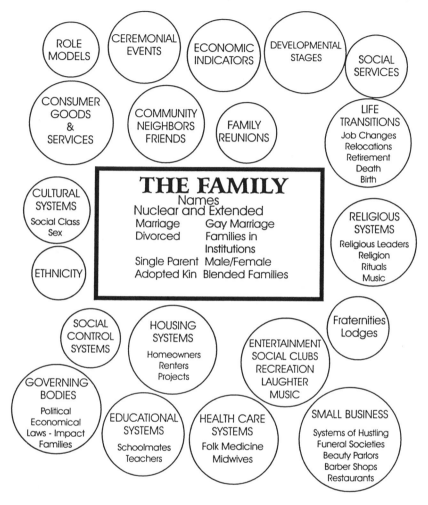

Figure 4.1. Ecological Map: Oral History Research Variables

SOURCE: Adapted from "Diagrammatic Assessment of Family Relationships," by A. Hartman, 1978, *Social Casework, 59*, p. 469. Used by permission from Family Service America, Inc., and A. Hartman.

(personal communication, January 19, 1995) recommends using two tape recorders when conducting interviews. This method serves two purposes: It guards against mechanical failure and provides a backup copy.

Researchers should record the name of the person being interviewed, date and place of interview, and label each tape. It is best to collect no more than one participant's interview on a tape. Researchers should come prepared with the following: (a) cassette (check to make sure it is working); (b) wall adapter and extension cord (some researchers such as Stave said "I no longer bother with these electrical backups—I come with extra batteries"); (c) extra batteries; (d) informed consent forms; and (e) notepad to take notes and to record proper spelling of difficult names.

Researchers should purchase cassette tapes of good quality and of medium time length. A 90-minute tape best suits the purpose of recording interviews. An hour and a half is also about the maximum length the average person will withstand such an interview. I have conducted interviews that have lasted from 3 to 4 hours, however. Some participants have taken the opportunity to prepare full meals; others have made lunches and served tea and cakes. For further discussion of this process, see Chapter 6.

ETHICAL CONSIDERATIONS
IN DATA COLLECTION

Ethical principles are guidelines that help researchers achieve and uphold values in research. These principles are essential to active researchers. These human participant guidelines also help to ensure that research is directed toward worthwhile research goals and that the welfare of project participants is protected. The most basic guideline for applied social scientists to adhere to is that the participant is not harmed by participation in the research. In addition to the ethical guidelines for applied research, each profession has a code of ethics. Therefore, I, a social worker, adhere to the National Association of Social Workers code of ethics, which complements my own values and respect for the respondents I interview.

INFORMED CONSENT

In research that entails the use of human participants, ethical principles require that interviewees be apprised of what the research entails. In my conduct of research, prior to beginning interviews, I explain to the participants why I am interested in their stories, what plans I have for the research, and that I wish to tape the interviews. Informed consent forms, which spell out the details of the research, are presented in duplicate for their signatures (see Appendix 4.1).

Another method I sometimes use, which is widely used by others, such as Stave, is that of getting permission before taping, transcribing the tape, slightly editing the transcript, returning the manuscript to the participant for review, and finally having the participant sign a second informed consent form. I have gotten mixed reaction from this process. For example, when I gave one participant the transcribed tape for this review, he was surprised and embarrassed that he had made so many grammatical errors.

The informed consent form, which I discuss with participants in detail, describes the nature of the research and the intended use of the research. I tell participants of the possibly harmful effects, if any, that may occur from the stirring up of feelings. The interviewees are informed that they are free to participate or to discontinue participation at any time. Any financial remunerations to be offered should also be discussed.

A good deal of mistrust of researchers may be found in groups in the African American community and other groups who have been left out, put down, and abused by the system, such as people who are poor or physically challenged, elderly persons, minorities, children, and newcomers who might have had to keep secrets to stay alive. Gwaltney (1980) described the care with which the African American community evaluates researchers. Credentials were not the only criteria, nor was race. Groups who have been abused, maligned, and lied to are not waiting with open arms to be exploited by educated White or African American researchers. Gwaltney found that the opinion of a reputable member of the community proved more valuable than purely professional credentials:

> A proper regard for security and reciprocity are vital to the establishment of rapport in core Black enclaves. The prudent are wary and slow to bestow confidence. Rapport is, generally, merited grace that is accorded by people who, in their considered judgment, have decided that the would-be researcher is not just another jackleg educated fool. (p. xxiv)

Like Gwaltney, I learned that I needed to be open to personal questions. I see the beauty and caring of the people when they say at the end of the interviews, "If we can be of any help, just call us."

HOW MUCH DO I TELL?

There is considerable discussion about how much to tell the participants about the research. I believe in being honest and aboveboard with my participants. But two summers ago, an incident made me realize that I had told so much that I confused my participants. I had interviewed a prominent, respected member of the community. When I presented the informed consent for her signature, she commented on the complicated, lengthy consent form, noting that she generally just signs a few lines granting people permission to do their research. She did in no way refuse to sign the form. In fact, she did so graciously.

I met with the next participants—husband, wife, and their two adult children who came to their parents' home to be interviewed also. As I prepared to set up my video equipment, I produced the consent form and told them about the incident at the previous interview. This family was reluctant to be interviewed. Finally, we got past my blunder and enjoyed an excellent interview. At the end, we all agreed that it had not been a painful experience after all.

We then processed what happened in the beginning. I had not stopped to think that if someone as knowledgeable, well-educated, and respected in the community as the first participant was reluctant to sign the consent form, others in the community would have concern and might hesitate to sign. I had failed to apply my own knowledge of what entry into Black communities is like.

In these days when camcorders are readily available and many people own them, oral history can be videotaped as well as audiotaped. Although the examples in this book refer to audiotapes, I have also found it helpful to capture on videotape pictures of historical spots, family gatherings, documents, and other archival materials. I sometimes use these as a complement to audiotapes, which I use primarily as the raw materials for transcription and analysis.

In the rest of this chapter, I will discuss the processes of transcribing and editing oral history tapes. (The remaining steps of analyzing, interpreting, and writing are covered in Chapter 5.) In some ways, the researcher actually begins this process while still conducting the interview, by informing the narrator as to the purpose of the research, how it will be used, and, probably, whether the researcher will transcribe the data onto sheets of paper and return to the interviewee for editing purposes. As the researcher proceeds with the interviews, he or she probably recognizes certain themes developing and may make some preliminary analysis and interpretation of the data.

TRANSCRIBING THE DATA

Transcribing the data is Step 8 of the 11-step process. Here is where the researcher sits down to a typewriter or computer, listens to the tape, and types the information that is on the tape onto sheets or reams of paper. These become the *narratives*. The researcher should prepare a typed manuscript in double or triple space, allowing room to make corrections between the lines or in the margins.

The decision whether to transcribe the tapes will depend on their expected uses. Although transcription is almost always a costly and time-consuming step, there are several reasons to transcribe. First, transcripts are easier to use than tapes. Finding, retaining, categorizing, and regrouping the information are much less time-consuming and often more accurate with a written record. Second, transcripts are useful for disseminating material to the wider public. This may be especially important if the work is to be used by others to fill in historical gaps, to sensitize others to how underrepresented or maligned groups view their experiences, or to collect baseline data. The third reason may be even more important to data collectors. Practitioners and students learn from transcribing their taped interviews, and the skills learned are not only about the narrators. Transcribers may find themselves improving their own interviewing and listening and may also learn to detect personal bias and personal blinders as they record the data and hear the interviews anew.

WHAT TO TRANSCRIBE

Transcribe everything. What researchers transcribe, however, depends on the uses to which the material will be put. Sometimes choosing not to transcribe may result in loss of important material. Yet sometimes, effectiveness may have to be considered. If time and resources are available, each tape should be transcribed. If an interview does not go well, a transcribed tape will help detect what went wrong in the interview. It also provides an opportunity to see if names and dates are correct.

Having a grant further enhances the option to transcribe. Professional services are also a good way to go. For example, researchers across the country use "Tapescribe," the transcribing services of the Center for Oral History at the University of Connecticut. Some participants are anxious to hear how they sound on the tape, therefore transcribing the tape gives them the opportunity to do so.

When time and resources are limited (transcribing is time-consuming, and a student could easily spend 8 to 10 hours transcribing a tape), researchers may elect not to transcribe—or to transcribe only portions, especially if a typist is unavailable. The steps in preparing a 90-minute interview can total 50 to 55 hours or maybe more. Emerson (1993) transcribed all three of her interviews. Class members discussed the trials and tribulations of the lengthy transcribing process. Believe me, I took a bit of "heat" from students at this point in the research process.

Although the tapes are transcribed, the value of the voice tone, language, and flavor cannot be overly stressed. I therefore see the need for both the tape and the transcribed narrative. I often assign students to break into groups to listen to, discuss, and analyze the tapes.

It is extremely frustrating to listen to a tape each time researchers want information about their research. If the tapes are not transcribed, researchers should index the tapes as soon as possible by using a table of contents or the library card catalog method. Other researchers have used the tape counter numbers to identify the location of themes on the tapes.

It is possible to transcribe (as I have done on occasion) from any tape recorder simply by hand operating the forward, stop, and reverse buttons and laboriously writing by hand the information onto pads of papers. Not only is this process slow and hard on the tape recorder, it is definitely hard on the hands. The transcriber will most likely need carpal tunnel surgery. I recommend a much more progressive method: a transcribing machine, which has a foot control for forward, stop, and reverse. It also has a variable speed control, which allows the transcriber to slow down the tape as needed. Included with the transcribing machine is a set of headphones, which are comfortable to wear because they come with foam ear cushions.

WHO SHOULD TRANSCRIBE

When I first began my research and began to search for a transcriber, I was sure that all I needed was a typist. I have since come to realize that much more is required. The transcriber becomes almost as intimately involved with the narrator as does the interviewer. It is important, therefore, that the transcriber (a) be patient, (b) have good listening skills, (c) be able to understand the nuances of the language of different cultures, (d) have a keen auditory ear for listening to electronic frames, and (e) possess good typing skills.

The best transcriber-editor is often the interviewer. The more the person knows about the research and the population, the better able he or she is to follow the tape. When the labor is free, such as a secretarial pool in a secretarial training program, it may be financially and expediently profitable to accept the offer. The interviewer will need to listen to the tapes again and fill in the gaps.

Transcribing, like conducting the oral history, is a work of art. The transcriber, like the interviewer, also must learn to translate from one language to another. If the transcriber is not the same as the interviewer, the transcriber has only the spoken word to convey what is on the tape. Voice, pitch, tone, feelings, strength of speakers, and language can only be imagined and all conveyed on the tape, but these are difficult to translate on paper with a great degree of accuracy.

I have found it helpful to use a transcriber who uses the narrator's words rather than substituting her or his own words. My regular transcriber also replays the tape, listening closely for broken sentences and presenting them in the language of the narrator. Another transcriber I have used on occasion is most meticulous, adding each "oh" and "uh" and whether the narrator and interviewer are laughing. She even includes the degree of laughter, noting whether either or both interviewer and interviewee are laughing loudly, chuckling, or "cracking up." The researcher should instruct the transcriber regarding how much of this detail to include.

My transcribers have said that they play parts of the tape before beginning to type. This helps acquaint them with the manner of speech. If they have missed some words, they go back later, listen again, and are likely to hear something they had not heard before. This avoids the inadvertent editing of items in or out prior to transcription.

EDITING

This is perhaps one of the areas that present the most difficulty. Oral historians disagree among themselves as to what should be edited in or out. Some believe the transcript should be an accurate and complete representation of what is on the tape. Others argue that the transcription should be edited into a smooth narrative, easy to follow by the narrative's user. I recommend beginning by transcribing the tape verbatim. This, after all, is that person's story as he or she sees it, feels it, and tells it. If the transcription will be essentially raw data for other researchers to use, the editing should be minimal. For example, the transcriber may remove false starts such as "uhs," "ahs," and stuttering—but with care. What may seem a stutter may be a statement of emphasis. If necessary, the transcriber should first write the word *stuttering* and put it in parentheses in the right location.

Recently I interviewed a narrator who was foreign-born (see Chapter 7). In reality, he was attempting to grasp the English word, which meant that the "uhs" and "ahs" were his reality at the time. His speech represented the areas in which he still needed mastery. This may be valuable data in a manuscript about coping, adaptation, and mastery in a new environment. It may be irrelevant to other uses of the material. Sometimes I have corrected grammar; other times I have not. How do I justify changing the language of an illiterate person? I do so if I feel that this is essential for a reader's comprehension. But I strive hard to avoid changing the meaning. The deciding factor is the researcher's intended use of the manuscript. To make sure I do not lose important material, I often make additional copies of the transcribed tapes before they are edited. These may be useful for both teaching and archival purposes.

As practitioners and educators, I believe we can make a case for both heavy editing and no editing. When the verbatim text is coherent, the narrative can be used in its entirety. It can be typed up indented in block form on the pages or framed on both sides. This manner of handling text allows the narrators to speak for themselves in their own words. This manner also allows for analyzing the data and interpreting the narratives.

Appendix 4.1

INFORMED CONSENT FORM

This is a research project being conducted by me in the Black community. The purposes are to contribute to our understanding of Black urban life in Tampa from the turn of the 20th century, to preserve the history of an ethnic group, to identify variables that may be utilized as a model for building leadership potentials of Black youth, and to leave a legacy to our youth of the next century. All interviews will be taped and later transcribed for purpose of publication. There is no risk.

I am asking your participation in the project. Participation is voluntary. You are free to refuse to participate and to discontinue participation at any time.

Confidentiality of the tapes and transcripts will be protected. I as sole owner will keep them in a locked file until the conclusion of the project. They will not be made available to anyone. The original research will involve ten to fifteen families.

The University has filed an Institutional Assurance with DHHS to assure the protection of human subjects, and a copy of this assurance will be made available upon request to the Division of Sponsored Research, University of South Florida.

If you have any pertinent questions about this research project, either during or after, you may reach me as follows:

> Dr. Ruth R. Martin
> College of Social & Behavioral Sciences
> Department of Social Work
> SOC 107
> Tampa, FL 33612
> Phone: 813-974-2063

Agree

_____   _____
Name of Participant   Date

REFERENCES

Atherton, C. R., & Klemmack, D. L. (1982). *Research methods in social work: An introduction.* Lexington, MA: D. C. Heath.

Babbie, E. (1983). *The practice of social research* (3rd ed.). Belmont, CA: Wadsworth.

Emerson, K. (1993). *Primary themes/topics from interviews with three women with breast cancer: Considerations of process in the making of meaning.* Student research project at the University of Connecticut, School of Social Work, West Hartford.

Gilligan, C. (1984). *In a different voice: Psychological theory and women's development.* Cambridge, MA: Harvard University Press.

Glaser, B., & Strauss, A. L. (1967). *The discovery of grounded theory.* New York: Aldine.

Green, J. W. (1982). *Cultural awareness in the human services.* Englewood Cliffs, NJ: Prentice Hall.

Gwaltney, J. L. (1980). *Drylongso: A self-portrait of Black America.* New York: Random House.

Hartman, A. (1978). Diagrammatic assessment of family relationships. *Social Casework, 59,* 465-476.

Lewis, O. (1963). *The children of Sanchez: Autobiography of a Mexican family.* New York: Random House.

Martin, R. R. (1987). Oral history in social work education: Chronicling the Black experience. *Journal of Social Work Education, 23*(3), 5-10.

Martin, R. R. (1988). Black family adaptation, survival and growth strategies: An oral history research project. In A. Rogers (Ed.), *Black family at the crossroads of development* (pp. 80-113). Columbia: University of South Carolina, College of Social Work.

Martin, R. R. (1991, August). *Life forces of African American elderly illustrated through oral history narratives.* Paper presented at a conference on Qualitative Methods in Social Work Research Practice, State University of New York at Albany, School of Social Welfare, Nelson A. Rockefeller Institute of Government.

Miles, M. B. (1983). Qualitative data as an attractive nuisance: The problem of analysis. In J. Van Maanen (Ed.), *Qualitative methodology* (pp. 117-134). Beverly Hills, CA: Sage.

Taylor, S. J., & Bogdan, R. C. (1984). *Introduction to qualitative research and methods: The search for meaning* (2nd ed.). New York: John Wiley.

Van Maanen, J. (1983). The fact of fiction in organization ethnography. In J. Van Maanen (Ed.), *Qualitative methodology* (pp. 37-55). Beverly Hills, CA: Sage.

5

ANALYZING AND INTERPRETING
DATA AND WRITING UP THE PROJECT

Analyzing and interpreting the data are Step 10 in the oral history process. The data have now been collected, the tapes transcribed, and researchers find that they have pages and pages of narratives. They will wonder how to bring some form and order to this evidence and how to make this material accessible. This process is called analysis (Bogdan & Biklen, 1992; Moss, 1984; Strauss & Corbin, 1990) or interpretation (Borland, 1991; Chanfrault-Duchet, 1991; Salazar, 1991; Thompson, 1978; Vansina, 1984).

ANALYSIS

"Analysis involves working with data, organizing them, breaking them into manageable units, synthesizing them, searching them, searching for patterns, discovering what is important and what is to be learned, and deciding what you will tell others" (Bogdan & Biklen, 1992, p. 153). Further, analysis goes far beyond the simple collection, preservation, and retrieval of information and beyond mere description. Analysis requires the comparing and testing of different records against each other, weighing the relative values of insight and evidence that they contribute in fair proportion, forming theoretical structures from the information (both evidence and insights), and then testing these new hypotheses against the evidence again and again to see if they can survive critical examination (Moss, 1984). Moss contends, however, that analysis inevitably has a limited perspective on the basis of the purposes for which the analysis was performed and the subjective interests of those performing the analysis.

But analysis can be fair and honest if all the evidence has been accounted for, the hypotheses rigorously tested, and the author's bias well defined and accounted for in the process.

Emerson (1993) organized themes and topics to depict the final analysis of the data from her project on women with breast cancer. She divided the data into three subheadings: overall listings, patterns, and the process of giving meaning to the experience. She organized the data and broke them into manageable units. Not only did she list these themes to illustrate how one does this, but she included selected narratives in support of these themes. Finally, she developed a chart to depict the methods she used for compilation of the work. These are displayed in Appendixes 5.1 through 5.4 of this chapter. Emerson's analysis is based on only three interviews. When these are combined with all other interviews and are based on thorough interviews of these women's perspective, however, her research has real value.

In my research, I find that I begin to analyze data while I am still conducting the research. Bogdan and Biklen (1992) describe 10 steps to interpret data while still in the field:

1. Force yourself to make decisions that narrow the study.
2. Force yourself to make decisions concerning the type of study you want to accomplish.
3. Develop analytic questions.
4. Plan data collection sessions in light of what you find in previous observation.
5. Write many "observer's comments" about ideas you generate.
6. Write memos to yourself about what you are learning.
7. Try out ideas and themes on subjects.
8. Begin exploring the literature while you are in the field.
9. Play with metaphors, analogies, and concepts.
10. Use visual devices.

In the project on Black family adaptation described in Chapter 6, I began to hear themes of racial barriers or racism. Racism became almost a given throughout the interviews. When interviewing one participant, I suggested that history seemed to say that Blacks experienced racism in Tampa from the turn of the century until the 1960s. She responded, "I never had any trouble with White people." She then proceeded within the next 20 minutes to give me examples of slights she experienced. In one such example, she described how she tried to borrow a book from the five-and-dime store that served as the town library but was denied because Blacks were not permitted to check books out. She later purchased a copy of the book for herself. I was somewhat puzzled by her earlier statement of not having "any trouble with White people." Later, as I transcribed the tape and read the narratives, I realized that I had not paid close attention to Step 3 as discussed in Chapter 4. I had not developed the analytic questions well enough. Luckily, my analytic skills were developed enough for me to recognize that the participant never said she had not experienced racism; she said "I never had any trouble." Had I explored further, she might have defined "trouble" as verbal confrontation, physical encounters, arrests, or the like.

Analyzing data after collection will certainly be easier if attention has been paid to the steps discussed previously. When I read the transcripts-narratives, however, I am always ambivalent whether I should go beyond reporting the narratives. I question how I can improve on or interpret someone else's perception of his or her reality. I, like Vansina (1984), realize that

> the layman is too often inclined to entertain a completely false idea as to the powers of the historian, and is apt to regard any historical reconstruction offered as absolutely valid. He fondly imagines that written sources reveal events of the past which can be accepted as fact but considers that oral sources tell of things about which there is no certainty—things which may or may not have happened. He forgets that any historical synthesis comprises an interpretation of facts, and is thus founded upon probabilities. (p. 104)

With these thoughts in mind, I begin my analysis by reading the narratives over several times (it helps if there are others who can read the narratives and help with the analysis). As I read and detect similar or new themes, I make notes on the margins of the paper. Examples of the themes Emerson isolated are listed in Appendix 5.2.

ORGANIZATION OF THEMES AND TOPICS

In a note related to a class assignment on her research project, Emerson (personal communication, April 11, 1993) discussed her attempts at organizing and making sense of the material. She wrote, "Isolating and separating themes didn't work for me; doesn't feel good to leave some out, not do justice to them; needed some glue (relationships and patterns)." (See Appendixes 5.1 to 5.4.)

CODING

Another method of analysis is referred to as *coding*. Imagine that a stock clerk in a drugstore must sort crates of decongestants that are all mixed up. There are many ways to sort them, and the clerk is certain to become confused by attempting to sort them on the basis of the claims for cure. If not familiar with brand names, the clerk is even more confused. Should the drugs be stocked according to colors or by pharmaceutical brands? The clerk develops a system, chooses to sort them into piles, and then counts how many are in a pile. This is considered coding. I give an example of the coding of restraining forces and survival strategies in Chapter 6. Emerson reported her analysis by organizing the narratives into themes and topics and then dividing the listing into patterns (see appendixes at the end of this chapter).

I sometimes conduct frequency counts from the narratives, and where appropriate, these are computed. Themes from the participants' narratives are presented in an attempt to understand what meanings are attached to driving and restraining forces; what nutrients are available and used for adaptive growth; and what advice would be beneficial for learners, educators, and community members to help them attain goodness of fit (adaptability with their environment).

INTERPRETATION

Earlier, I discussed the logical analysis of data. Once researchers have performed the analysis, they must still interpret the analysis. Interpretation, Vansina (1984) argues,

> is a choice between several possible hypotheses (assumptions), and the good historian is the one who chooses the hypothesis (assumption) that is most likely to be true. . . . In practice it can never have more than a likelihood of truth, because the past has gone for good. . . . There is no such thing as "absolute historical truth" and no one can formulate an unchanging law of history on the basis of our knowledge of the past. (pp. 105-106)

It has been my experience to interview participants who truly have been a part of the past events for which I have attempted to gain a historical knowledge. And even though I sometimes agree with Vansina (1984) that the "truth always remains beyond our grasp," I continue to attempt to refine my interpretations with the hope that I will arrive at some approximation of historical truth. I do this by "interpreting the facts and by evaluating them in an attempt to recreate for [myself] the circumstances . . . at certain given moments of the past" (p. 106).

Nevertheless, Vansina (1984) makes a case for the validity of oral history by arguing that the researcher who uses the oral traditions "finds himself on exactly the same level as historians using any other kind of historical source material" (p. 106). Although oral history researchers will arrive at a lower degree of "probability" (Vansina contends that all history is no more than a calculation of probabilities) than would otherwise be attained, it does not invalidate what we do. It is history.

Borland (1991) raises the issue of possible misinterpretation of narratives that are collected in an article in which she, in effect, tells on herself. Borland described how her grandmother, Beatrice, reacted to the feminist slant that Borland gave to her account of a day in 1944. As a young woman, Beatrice, who had opted for the rarely used avenue of divorce to leave a marriage, attended the horse races with her father, the lawyer who handled her divorce, and his son. Protocol in this conservative Maine community called for the men to place bets for the women, who were generally expected to root for the same horses as their men. Beatrice not only chose to bet but also put her money behind a horse whose chances were ridiculed by her father. She ignored his contempt and allowed the amused lawyer's son to place her bet on this and two other horses to which her father objected. She won each time. Borland wrote an analysis that found much feminist rebellion as indicated by her grandmother's divorce and behavior at the races. When her grandmother read the materials, she wrote,

> Your interpretation of the story as a female struggle for autonomy within a hostile male environment is entirely *your* interpretation. You've read into the story what you wished to—what pleases *you*. . . . The story is no longer *my* story at all. The skeleton remains, but it has become your story. Right? How far is it permissible to go, in the name of folklore, and still be honest in respect to the original narrative? (Borland, 1991, p. 70)

Beatrice later acknowledged that although she had never embraced the feminist movement in her day or in modern times, she lived out its ideals. Nonetheless, Borland realized that she should have asked the narrator about her interpretation of meaning before imposing her own as a researcher.

Researchers can also be hasty and interpret data before they have taken time to clearly understand what is being said. For example, when I interviewed Slava (Chapter 7), he described the difficulties he experienced in the migration process, including how he applied in Rome for entrance into the United States and was initially denied, thereby being unsure of his fate. I wondered if he were frightened because of his situation, and he responded that he was not frightened because he had a choice to go to Israel. I interpreted this from the position that when human beings are given choices, given some opportunity to participate in decisions about their lives, they become empowered. This flaw in interpretation was poignantly called to my attention by one of my readers. He wrote that "a good clinician would wonder how you arrived at the conclusion that Slava really had a choice. It might just be that he felt secure about going to Israel even if this was not his first choice." Naturally, I reread the narrative and my interpretation. I then questioned how, despite also considering myself a good clinician, I had made such an obvious error in interpretation.

Looking back and inward, I realized that I had hurriedly made an interpretation by viewing the narrative through my own cultural lens. This example reiterates the need to view the narrative from the narrator's perspective. It also demonstrates that attempting to view the meaning of one's world through another's requires considerable effort. In Chapter 7, I present an opportunity for readers to interpret Slava's meaning. "Remember, there is usually more than one interpretation possible" (Vansina, 1984, p. 106).

Step 10 asks that the researcher-educator-learner make some statement as to what has been learned from the study. Is there a need for further research? How can this be applied to practice or to change social policy? If she had it to do over again, Emerson (personal communication, November 26, 1993) says she would (a) ask participants to clarify what about the experience empowered them (i.e., go into it in more detail) and (b) like to check her reading of the information with respondents in relation to their own meaning. She also said that she learned that interviews can build on each other and should be used in this way.

WRITING UP THE PROJECT

Reporting research serves an important function in social work. In earlier chapters, I argued that oral histories can add to the knowledge base of the profession. Writing up the report can facilitate the dissemination of this knowledge and communicate to others the knowledge gained from the research projects.

As I have written up my research findings for publication in professional journals, for conference and television presentations, for monographs for community use, and for reports for agency use, I find that each write-up is different. More specifically, when I wrote up my first major research project, my purpose was to share the research with the Black community about the adaptive capacities of its own unsung heroes and heroines. Therefore, I presented the material at the town's public library and a more detailed written report at a conference on the Black family (see Chapter 6 of this book). Excerpts from the narrative were also presented during Black History Month celebrations at a conference on the Black family sponsored by my church, at the veterans hospital, and at the University of South Florida.

The write-up and the tapes that accompany the manuscript often serve as a teaching tool. When I am forced to condense the manuscript from 40 pages to 25 pages or less for journal publication consideration, however, I find the effort exceedingly difficult. I feel strongly that each concern or narrative is valuable. I also struggle with ethical issues such as I discussed under Steps 7 and 8. Have I the right to decide individual meanings of the participants? In Chapter 9 on adolescent pregnancy, I present a revised example of a research project written for journal publication.

Researchers often wish to write up their projects for both journal and community use. Sometimes this becomes extremely challenging. This was especially true when I attempted to write up the project on the Pliny Street Block Association (Chapter 10). When the researchers and I received permission to interview the participants of Pliny Street, we promised to provide them with a final report. When I, as editor, finally wrote the full report, I reasoned that out of respect for the community and the participants, I would need to write a lengthier report than if I wrote for a journal article. Therefore, even allowing for condensing the narratives, the manuscript turned out to be more than 110 pages. My hunch was correct, however. For when I met with the association to share the results, they were enthusiastic about the report. They said they never expected the report to be of such good quality. Some members turned immediately to the narrative section, looking to see what they and their neighbors said in the interviews. I said, "I knew you were going to look to see who said what, but I deliberately left the names off." We all shared in the laughter. A few of the members admitted that they were able to identify some of the narrators by what was said. Because the full text of this final product could not conceivably be considered for this book, Chapter 10 presents a condensation of the report.

The purpose of this chapter and Chapter 4 was to discuss the process and method of oral history research. I have illustrated with examples the 11 steps that I use in the process.

In Part II of this book, Chapters 6 through 10 contain oral history projects that I have written up. They are based on studies employing the methodology outlined in this book. They provide a sense of some of the diverse issues that can be addressed and give readers examples of how to write up their own findings.

Appendix 5.1

SELECTED QUOTES FROM
INTERVIEWS IN SUPPORT OF THEMES

INITIAL REACTIONS

Gladys: First it was shock, then I was really, really surprised, and then I think, I didn't think it was really going to happen. It was shock, disbelief, anger, scared to death.

Diane: I felt a scaring kind of pain down . . . I just felt this . . . I can't describe it; it was like a dead-plunk, kind of; I was like up against this wall, staring at this huge wall. I think it was sheer panic.

Connie: Well, I just didn't know how to react. I remember thinking, "This isn't me; it can't be real."

INTEGRATION

Diane: I guess the disease has been a gift in terms of . . . hey, it's like, I've had cancer, I can say and do whatever I want. Not really, but there is some of that. I really feel that I was at the door so many times, I mean of being more afraid than I've ever been in my life, realizing that this could be absolute, that I might not be here, depending on what happens. And I still carry some of that absoluteness about the day, about my son, and being present in things I want to be and not being present in things I don't want to be, that I can really pick and choose the things that I want to put my time into now.

Gladys: I'm taking better care of myself. I'm realizing that life itself is very fragile and I think I am trying to live in a different kind of. . . . I can understand and love other people better because I now love myself. . . . I'm more in touch with myself.

Connie: I think my life is richer and it's between my retirement and my cancer. It would be hard to sort out. You know, I'm sorry it happened but . . .

GETTING INFORMATION

Gladys: I need to talk about it and think about it. The first thing I did was decide that I needed a second opinion. And I did a lot of reading. . . . [And at the end] gather your resources together, gather your books around you, gather your friends around you and find the best medical help that you can.

Diane: At that point I think I bought and borrowed every possible article and book, anything I could read. I talked to everybody I was given a phone number for. It was just this intense program of trying to . . . I guess empower myself. I needed information before I could make a decision. . . . It was like a crash course in cancer.

Connie: We joined the library and got what reading I could. Our instinct was to find out all we could.

"MAKING IT MINE"

Connie: It's hard for me to remember because I actually had begun to assimilate it sooner. . . . My head was getting used to the fact that I had a problem. . . . So, in a sense, I was already beginning to take it in that I had a problem, [and] . . . the times when you wake up in the middle of the night and you are sure you are having recurrence, or you're driving down the road and for some reason it just starts going through your head, wondering about those little things crawling around in your body. I knew that I would have to realize that from now on that everything that happened to me I would have to run cancer by it.

Diane: The realization that every waking minute of the day that "I have cancer, I have cancer" and (at first) not being able to push it away, not being able to think of anything else.

BELIEFS ABOUT CAUSE

Gladys: I do believe strongly about the emotional part of your life, when it falls apart that other things happen. I have a tendency to be a person who holds my feelings, my emotions, especially anger and rage and stuff, inside, and I think that it's not good for one.

SOURCE: Developed by K. Emerson (1993). Reprinted by permission.

Appendix 5.2

ORGANIZATION OF
THEMES AND TOPICS

OVERALL LISTING

Early reactions
Decision-making
Taking control
Choosing for self
Boundaries
Getting information
Getting support
Wholeness
Balance
Life is precious
Nonpersonhood
Awakening/rebirth
Support systems
Others' needs

Religion/spirituality
Strength/weakness
Getting strong
Role of emotions
Emotional/physical balance
Beliefs about cause
Empowerment
Alternative treatments
Self-image
Loss
Death/dying
Living
Growing trust in self
Getting a voice

New expressiveness
Journals
Lifelong learning
Learning to say no
Taking time for self
Surviving
Daughters
Sisters
Support from men/women
Importance of eyes and voice
Positive aspects of disease
Change and growth
Control/lack of control
Paradox
Making a meaning
Integration of experience

SOURCE: Developed by K. Emerson (1993). Reprinted by permission.

Appendix 5.3

PATTERNS

A process	Reevaluation of responsibilities
A journey	Modes and styles of expression
Learning to value self apart from others	Differences before/after cancer
Life as waking sleep	Active meaning making
Sick, dead self	Stages in this process
Surviving	Formation of new kinds of relationships
Getting strong	Disease as catalyst
Strategies to get/stay well	Learning to say no
Creating new self	Gaining a voice

SOURCE: Developed by K. Emerson (1993). Reprinted by permission.

Appendix 5.4

CHOOSING FINAL CATEGORIES REFLECTING THESE PATTERNS AND THE PROCESS OF GIVING MEANING TO THE EXPERIENCE

Initial Reactions
"Making It Mine"
Beliefs re: Causes
Getting Information
Getting Support
"Others" and Self
Gaining a Voice
Integration/Empowerment
Surviving
Here and Now
New Relationships
Rebirth

SOURCE: Developed by K. Emerson (1993). Reprinted by permission.

REFERENCES

Bogdan, R. C., & Biklen, S. K. (1992). *Qualitative research for education: An introduction to theory and methods* (2nd ed.). Boston: Allyn & Bacon.

Borland, K. (1991). That's not what I said: Interpretive conflict in oral narratives research. In S. B. Gluck & D. Patai (Eds.), *Women's words: The feminist practice of oral history* (pp. 63-75). New York: Routledge, Chapman & Hall.

Chanfrault-Duchet, M. S. (1991). Narrative structures, social models and symbolic representation in the life stories. In S. B. Gluck & D. Patai (Eds.), *Women's words: The feminist practice of oral history* (pp. 77-92). New York: Routledge, Chapman & Hall.

Emerson, K. (1993). *Primary themes/topics from interviews with three women with breast cancer: Considerations of process in the making of meaning.* Student research project at the University of Connecticut, School of Social Work, West Hartford.

Moss, W. (1984). Oral history: An appreciation. In D. K. Dunway & W. K. Baum (Eds.), *Oral history: An interdisciplinary anthology* (pp. 87-101). Nashville, TN: American Association for State and Local History.

Salazar, C. (1991). A third world women's text: Between the politics of criticism and cultural politics. In S. B. Gluck & D. Patai (Eds.), *Women's words: The feminist practice of oral history* (pp. 93-106). New York: Routledge, Chapman & Hall.

Strauss, A., & Corbin, J. (1990). *Basics of qualitative research: Grounded theory procedure and technique.* Newbury Park, CA: Sage.

Thompson, P. R. (1978) *The voice of the past: Oral history.* Oxford, UK: Oxford University Press.

Vansina, J. (1984). Oral tradition and historical methodology. In D. K. Dunway and W. K. Baum (Eds.), *Oral history: An interdisciplinary anthology* (pp. 102-106). Nashville, TN: American Association for State and Local History.

PART II
Examples of Oral History Research

In this section of the book, I present oral history projects using the 11-step process described in Chapters 4 and 5. Each oral history study illustrates, with varying emphasis on different steps, how to conduct an oral history project and to pull the findings together to share with the respondents and others. Three of these studies show how people who live with oppression cope and transcend. The oppression of African Americans and Russian Jews may seem worlds apart, yet some of the coping mechanisms and some of the issues are strikingly similar.

Oral history is also used to preserve the history of organizations and people in communities. The history of the settlement movement in Connecticut as it involves African Americans fills in the gaps in history that have been whitewashed by time and racist reporting of events. The history of the Pliny Street Block Association documents what African American people can do in a community. This section illustrates the many ways in which oral history research can build the knowledge base of the profession and also be of use to the general public.

6

BLACK FAMILY ADAPTATION, SURVIVAL, AND GROWTH STRATEGIES
An Oral History Project

In this chapter, I show how oral research was used to illuminate the strengths of Black families from the retrospective point of view of Black elders in the Gulf Coast city of Tampa, Florida. In Chapter 2, I discussed the multidimensional theoretical perspective that I used to guide my research on the Black family. In this chapter, I use the perspective to show the adaptive strengths of Black families. In addition, I include enough narrative data to view Black families through a "window" to their world, hear it from their own voices, and interpret it through their lenses. Through discussion of this project, I describe the procedural details of oral history study: the research design, purpose and objectives, rationale, sample selection, instrumentation, data collection procedures, and data analysis.

METHODOLOGY

RESEARCH DESIGN AND PARTICIPANTS

In this oral history project, I used an exploratory research design. The project focused on the adaptation of Black families as seen through the eyes of elder family members in a specific locale. Participants included

AUTHOR'S NOTE: The narratives in this chapter are from interviews conducted through the University of South Florida as part of a research project in Tampa, Florida, from 1982 through 1984 (see also Martin, 1987, 1988). Used with permission.

15 Black American families. Ages of the participants ranged mostly from 60 to 85 years.

PURPOSE AND OBJECTIVES

The project sought to

1. Preserve the history of an ethnic group
2. Contribute to the understanding of the meaning of Black family life in one locale from the turn of the 20th century to the mid-1980s
3. Identify community systems Black families use
4. Develop new knowledge of how Black families in this community transmit motivational and survival techniques
5. Identify role models
6. Identify variables that may be used as models for building leadership potentials for Black youth
7. Leave a legacy to Black youth of the next century

The main purpose of the project was to learn about Black family adaptation and survival.

Like Lewis (1963), I believe I have avoided the two most common hazards in the study of low-income Black people: sentimentalization and brutalization. I hope this study creates for readers a new excitement and dedication to an understanding of and sensitivity to the Black experience, people of color, and others who have been left out of formal systems.

RATIONALE FOR THE STUDY

In 1965, Moynihan described the structure of the Black family as disorganized, dysfunctional, and a "tangle of pathology" (p. 6) leading to highly unstable families. In 1987, Billingsley, noting many strengths, said that the African American family was still struggling for stability. In his most current work, Billingsley (1992) takes a fresh look at the age-old questions: Is the African American family vanishing? Is it a "tangle of pathology"? Is there an absence of family values? And what is the future of the African American family? He writes,

> A sufficiently broad and deep understanding of the Black experience in the world and in the nation will reveal that there are values and adaptive capacities as well as social, economic, and political structures, movements, and personages already in place attesting to the possibility of harnessing the enormous resources of this people, connecting them with the forces of the larger society in ways to make family life more viable. (p. 23)

As the researcher, I set out to record oral history from Blacks in this community who were born around the turn of this century. Topics included their motivations, the role of family in survival and coping, role models, aspirations, and most of all, how they adapted, survived, and often prospered in nonnutritive environments. Because there was no earlier research, I feared that the entire history of Blacks in this city during a most important period would be lost forever. Given the shorter average life expectancy of Blacks, the strong possibility existed that the participants would die, carrying this information with them to the grave. This would have tragically deprived future generations of a legacy of Black survival.

SAMPLE SELECTION, RELIABILITY, AND VALIDITY

The sampling process I used is called *snowballing*. This type of selection is discussed in Chapter 4 of this book. For the most part, one human connection led to many others.

A built-in check on the reliability and validity of much of the data was gained by the independent versions of many of the same incidents given by various participants and sometimes family members. For example, three siblings whose ages ranged from 65 years to 76 years were interviewed. They each discussed their father's determination that they should learn and their mother's determination that they would not work in the cigar industry. This research method of multiple autobiographies reduced the element of investigator bias because the accounts were not put through the sieve of the researcher's mind but were given in the words of the participants themselves. Although I have reduced the potential for investigator bias, other elements that could affect reliability include participants' memory or diminished importance of the incident, which may result in a new subjective view.

DATA-GATHERING INSTRUMENT

Structure for the interviews was provided by a slightly revised version of Hartman's eco-map (1978, p. 469), which I described more fully in Chapter 4. The eco-map, a simple paper-and-pencil simulation, maps the ecological system, including systems that provide a nutritive quality to Black family life as well as those that create barriers to Black adaptation. A copy of the eco-map was given to the participants to help them proceed at their own pace, recalling events that have certain meanings. The map also served as a checkpoint for the interviewees (as did a questionnaire I used), helping to organize their thoughts.

DATA COLLECTION

Once possible participants were identified by organizations or peers, individual interviews with couples and single parents were scheduled through telephone contact. Although 15 families constituted the sample, I conducted a total of 20 interviews. Some children of the next generation were interviewed but were not included in the analysis of this research.

Oral history interviews were time-consuming and sometimes tedious. They ranged from 2 to 5 hours. The elders were not always able to sustain such lengthy interviews; this required additional visits. Participants did not recall information in chronological order. Some events were dated by occurrences. For example, an elderly person clarified the date of birth of a niece whose birth certificate showed an October birthdate in this manner: "I know the exact month of her birth. She was born before I moved to Washington. I delayed my trip to Washington until my sister gave birth. So, I didn't get to leave until after Thanksgiving. That child was born in November, not in October" (interview, February 16, 1983). As previously mentioned, the eco-map helped the participants organize their cognitive mapping processes.

DATA ANALYSIS

This is Step 10 of the research project as described in Chapter 5. Because it is the most important conceptual work, I will describe and illustrate it more fully here. After the oral histories were tape-recorded and later transcribed, I reviewed the narratives for common themes and edited the data. Editing was necessary because of the failure of transcribers to understand some of the participants' speech patterns. Identifying adaptive, survival, and growth strategies was the desired outcome of this oral history project. No attempt was made to compare variables because only loose hypotheses were developed prior to the research. Frequency counts were taken from the transcribed tapes and were computed where appropriate. Themes from the participants' narratives were presented in an attempt to understand what nutrients were available and used for adaptive growth and to determine, given the current state of the Black family, what advice would be beneficial to Black youth of the next generation to help them attain goodness of fit.

ANALYSIS BY TABLE

In the sample of 20, 11 participants were married, 5 were widowed, 1 was separated, and 3 had never married (see Table 6.1). The participants

TABLE 6.1   Description of Participants by Marital Status

Marital History	Married Men	Married Women	Single Women	Single Men	Total
Never married			3		3
Separated				1	1
Divorced					
Widowed			4	1	5
Married	6	5			11
TOTAL					20

TABLE 6.2   Description of Participants by Age

Current Age	Married Men	Married Women	Single Women	Single Men	Total
Under 55		1			1
60-70	1	2			3
71-75	5	3		1	9
76-80	1	1	2		4
81-85			3		3
TOTAL					20

were from 60 years to 85 years old, except for one who was under 55 (see Table 6.2).

Most of the participants were retired. As was true of the majority of Blacks of that period, teaching was the major profession. At the time of the project, one respondent, age 82, went to work each day at one of her businesses, a nursing home. Another respondent, age 75, ran a day care center, and another, age 73, managed his real estate business. One 75-year-old interviewee volunteered to teach reading to Hispanic children. Others performed various volunteer, fraternal, and sorority functions (see Table 6.3). In addition, each participant was an active church member. With the exception of a second wife whose age was below 40, participants had been active in church for more than 40 years. Many started going regularly. Participants were affiliated with many Christian denominations, including African Methodist Episcopal, Episcopal, Catholic, Methodist, and Baptist.

In their interviews, participants related their perceptions of restraining environmental elements in their lives. Table 6.4 shows 16 themes that participants identified. One of the themes mentioned by all participants was racism. The interviewees conveyed that Blacks experienced a lack of

TABLE 6.3 Description of Participants by Occupation

Occupation	Married Men	Married Women	Widowed Women	Single Women	Divorced Men	Total
Health field/ nursing/retired		1	2			3
Railroad industry	1					1
Retired schoolteacher	1	2	2	3		8
Currently teaching		1				1
Retired lawyer, minister teaching	1					1
Retired principal/ real estate	2					2
Retired principal/ day care	1					1
Government	1	1			1	3
TOTAL						20

TABLE 6.4 Description of Participants' Perceptions of Restraining Forces

Characteristics

Racism
Capitalism (exploitation)
Lack of participation in the political system
Inadequate housing
Segregated school systems
Poor educational facilities
Effect of slavery still present
Segregation
Lack of central black leadership
Teenage pregnancy
Black on Black crime
Loss of teachers as role models
Blacks live in closed, isolated society
Races don't communicate with one another
Discrimination against Blacks in employment and businesses
Lack of power
Lack of role models in economics/business or schools

power, were not permitted to participate in the political system, and lived in a closed, isolated society. Participants cited additional restraining forces such as inadequate housing, crime, effects of slavery, and poor or nonnutritive educational systems.

TABLE 6.5   Adaptive and Survival Strategies Identified by Participants

Characteristics	Married Men	Married Women	Single Women	Single Men	Total
Strong family relationships	6	5	7	2	20
Strong primary support to family	6	5	7	2	20
High expectations from parents	6	5	7	2	20
Foundation of love	6	4	7	2	19
People needing/caring for each other	6	5	7	2	20
Strong work orientation	6	5	7	2	20
Discipline	6	5	7	2	20
Strong values	6	5	7	2	20
Friends treated as family	6	5	6	2	19
Community relies on each other	6	5	7	1	19
Ability to laugh at the outrageous	5	3	6	2	16
Strong family participation	6	5	3	2	16
Strong use of Black language/language	5	3	4	2	14
Active church participation	6	5	7	2	20
Strong role models	6	5	7	2	20

Table 6.5 lists the participants' perceptions of adaptive and survival strategies. When asked how families survived, more than 50% of the respondents, using a variety of descriptive terms, concluded that Black families had strong family relationships, strong relationships with friends who were often treated as family, love and high expectations from parents, strong work orientations, discipline, strong values, reliance on each other, active church participation, strong use of Black language, and the ability to laugh at the outrageous.

NARRATIVES DEPICTING
SURVIVAL STRATEGIES

The following narrative excerpts from the interviews illustrate several of the adaptive strategies shown in Table 6.5. Readers can see how the categorization of survival strategies was derived from the narratives. The first narrative is particularly revealing.

Well, you know, we had strong family ties—strong family networks. And I also feel it was a matter of survival in a sense. By that I mean this—Blacks had their own churches, lodges, amusement organizations, fellowship organizations, and we had found a niche in all of these spots. And we were happy. Most Blacks were happy to go to *his* church [respondent's emphasis]. And uh—you know, at that time the Blacks even had a second language. He talked one way within his own social group and another way when Whites were present. And these Whites didn't know.

But actually the White man in a sense was to be pitied because we were really content because we were living by the value system, and he wasn't. Therefore, he was psychologically schizophrenic in a sense, and he had to feel guilty in my presence when I didn't have to feel guilty in his presence. And that's why old mammy who was a domestic could laugh at sister Sue if you understand what I'm saying.

She'd get on the bus and go to Sister Sue's house every morning and she was more of a contented person than Sister Sue. Although Sister Sue carried the air of sophistication and superiority, in a sense she wasn't.

Because Sister Sue she assumed her role and old mammy played an inferior role in order to satisfy Sister Sue [example of behavior as an adaptive skill]. And that's one of the major reasons Blacks have survived. He wasn't foolish like the Indian. The American Indian wanted to stand up and buck him, and then he got shot down. But we would bow our heads and didn't mean it.

I asked the participants to identify strategies that would be helpful for the Black youth of today in their adaptations. Their responses are shown in Table 6.6.
The following narratives portray three participants' views of adaptive strategies regarding the importance of education, a strong economic base, and role models.

EDUCATION

Adaptation involves applying self, cultivating talents and a belief in solid values. This education is important—one must stay in school. Nothing has changed when it comes to standards. If one wants to become a college professor, he must go to school. He must meet the qualifications or he will never become a college professor. Nothing from the standpoint of getting ahead in America has changed. We must still apply ourselves, cultivate our talents, and believe in something. You gotta believe in something. And you

TABLE 6.6   Strategies Identified by Participants That May Be Used by Black Youth

Themes	Number of Times Mentioned
Kids must be taught to take advantage of parents' prosperity	2
Children lack the determination they once had to achieve—education must again become highly valued	19
We must apply and cultivate young talent	17
Black children need cohesion—need common goals	15
Black youth must have strong role models	20
Need to instill proper guidance	15
Structure and discipline must be given	20
Black youth should have employment	17
Teachers who care must teach	19
Teach them how to operate from an economic base	18
Black parents should visit their children in school to understand what is happening	18
Must teach Black youth to have an appreciation for what we have	19
We must teach Black youth about our history/culture	20
We must get it into our minds and into the minds of our youth that the best thing we have is that which we have ourselves	10
We tell our children what we fought to get, we don't tell them that they need to fight to hold it	20
The basis of helping Black youth is still help at home	20

gotta have some objectives. And uh, that is—nothing is going to get solved by getting high, or by frivolous frivolity. Not any of those things are going to put us into successful positions. (Narrator 1)

Our public schools are like the government system. It's there for you. It's there for you. Anything—as far as a good education you can get it in a public school, in a private school, or you can get it at home. If you want to. If you have the desire to get ahead. Uh, some of the finest people in the world are in these public schools. There was a study made of the top universities and uh, the major percentage of the better students in these top universities came out of the public schools. Public schools have made America.

It was through the public schools that we were able to lift our society. And it's gonna continue to be the instrument that lifts our people, White and Black. Now if—there is no easy road and when I say there is no easy road I mean that one has to still apply himself and cultivate the God-given talents he has. If he doesn't do that and he thinks there is pie in the sky he's losing his way. He's gotta have an objective and he's gotta believe. And the system is here just like our government.

It's a fine government. And our public school system is a fine system. But we can't—we've got to exploit. Now what I mean by that—I go to school, I got to listen to the teacher and not believe that some magical wand that she can wave and make me a successful person. She's there to be exploited, and if I don't exploit and don't believe that she is something that can help me then I'm not going to take advantage of the system. The public school system or any other system. That's my advice. (Narrator 2)

Narrator 3 describes thoughts about education and the need for children to have some connections with their roots.

I might hasten to add that you would be amazed to know what good jobs the schools are doing. It is easy to go into any classroom and start asking [students] questions. You'd be amazed at the many, many students who are profiting from attending our schools.

I tell you another problem we have, one disruptive child can neutralize the whole program. I was working with a boy before I dropped out with the flu (I think I'll start back this week) who had been a problem with everybody, every class he'd been to he'd been a terrible problem. He had a Latin name so I presumed by that that I would approach him from that angle. Then I discovered that he barely spoke English. I also discovered he was living in a foster home. He had five brothers and sisters and they were scattered around foster homes and from time to time he'd go visit them.

Now you could see that a child like that without any real roots is in big trouble. So we entered into kind of a tacit agreement that he would be my assistant and it gave him a sense of being someone to file my books for me, things like that. At least it kept him from disturbing other students.

Then it dawned upon me that I was treating him in a certain sense because, while keeping him busy kept him out of trouble, *I wasn't teaching him anything.* So I had to go back and devise a program for him and starting just on simple reading and writing. So then we had to make a second agreement that he would give me about 15 or 20 minutes of reading through the day. Now that sounds very good, like a success story. But you can't individualize your attention that much and still take care of other students. That's another problem that we have. (Narrator 3)

The participant continued by discussing what he thinks is the biggest change from when he was young. Much of his narrative shows themes of changes in mass society and how families are affected by and cope with those changes.

The biggest change has been in attitudes toward schools and education. Children just don't, well they don't have the regard for their teachers and education that they did in those days. Again, I'm not talking about the teacher who—what is the right term?—the hickory stick? I don't think you necessarily need corporal punishment. You see this is why I look back upon my parents with a sense of almost reverence because despite their paucity of formal training, they had such high ideals and such values. I could not open my mouth in Spanish or in English in my home unless I used the correct grammatical form.

My father was always interested in my education. There was hardly a time that he would not walk into the house and question me about what I had done in school that day. What did you do in school? What are you studying? He was a poorly trained man but he had acquired a lot of books. The minute I would tell him what I was studying, he'd go look it up and then he'd come with some questions. So we were brought up in such an academic atmosphere and the children today don't have that.

It isn't always a malignancy, it's a question of change. The civil rights revolution, of which I'm proud that I was a small part, got to be just like the French Revolution, you know, we're going to kill the masters who have plagued us with all these outrages. Then we start killing the masters, first off the masters, then we start killing ourselves. So we find that human rights first meant the rights of Black people to enjoy the American society, to which they fought.

But then it became also the rights of women, and I think it's a good thing. But when a child gets up in class and throws a spitball at another child, and you tell 'em don't do that, in a minute he's telling me his rights. Well, the teach hollered at me when I did it. She taught me my rights. We have prostituted, you see, the idea of human rights. Human rights now mean "My rights to do as I please. I don't give a damn what the consequences are." That's one of the big problems now.

In the narratives below, the participant tells us how to motivate Black youth and describes what is lacking and what youth need.

ECONOMIC BASE

Develop an economic base. If you are going to be a successful people, you have to try to move in those areas that would tend to build for yourself, and for your community—your constituency, this monetary base. Move together on your projects. There is no such thing as an individual anymore.

ROLE MODELS

They are disillusioned. And they are disillusioned because of something we discussed a while ago. They lack role models. They're disillusioned because even though segregation was very unfair—and I'm not for segregation—in their schools [meaning all-Black schools] they were able to be accepted along certain lines. Today they are just there. Oh, there are some outstanding Black students here . . . but the average kid doesn't have a chance. That's where the vacuum comes. We, as teachers, used to push our kids. One form of motivation was look, "You're going to have to be better—not as good— but better, in order to get along." That was hammered into his head, and that's how he saw it.

In the following narrative, this participant describes what role models provide. She also tells us that Blacks had different social classes. Her example shows that there were subgroups within the Black culture.

During my day, the majority of those people who wanted to be somebody, who wanted to go to college, they would socialize, mingle with people that were college people, you know. I don't mean to say that they were snobs, but those would be their main friends. Now take for instance, when those people would come back from school, you would always be with them, asking about school life. You would ask them what it was like, what happened, the things that they did. And all you could just do was see yourself there. One day. All you could do was say, "One day, I'll be right there."

This participant continues the discussion. She, like many of the participants, tells about parents who were strong role models. Schoolteachers were also role models. Further, these were students who cared about their classmates. They seem to give new definition to love for fellow human beings.

I remember when Roland Hayes came to Tampa, to perform a recital, I had to go. Anything of interest. I always wondered why I had to go. Later in life, I always thought this: Mother wanted me to go to hear and to see things that were important in life. She wanted me to see people who stood for something, that it would grow up in my mind to want to be like them, to want to do something, that's the only reason I feel that she never left me at home. She always carried me. And I was going to be like that, wanted to be like that. But you know, I tell you one thing, I believe our kids wouldn't carry so much hate in their hearts, they wouldn't be like they are if they were active with things like I did. Our kids carry a lot of anger.

When I was coming to school, there was always a teacher that we admired and wanted to be like. Our classes weren't as large as the classes today. But we didn't let our classmates just drop out, we would check up on them and say, "Why you don't come to school, what's wrong?" We'd go to see about 'em, we'd go check up on 'em, try to keep 'em in. They don't give a hoot about each other, care whether they come or not. But we'd go and check up on our classmates, we'd go check, go and see, "You weren't in school today, what's wrong?" One's grades be falling low, we would study together. "Come on, we've got to pull up, do better than that."

I had an algebra teacher, brother, you made an F (if you stayed out of class) and another the next week, you were gone in his class. We'd check on each other, we tried to help each other so we could all stay together. They don't think nothing about each other, they don't care nothing about grades. We knew we only had 6 days to stay out of class, a period, and you automatically would make an F. I was surprised when I was looking at the absentee list and saw all those absentees.

"Boy," I said, "wow, all these students absent from school in one day." In an all-Black school, the principal would have jumped down our throat. If we had that many students absent from school, he would have to do something. Call up or go out or do something—we never had that many children out in one day. He had to talk to them, stay on those kids and those parents, those kids stayed in school, especially in a colored school, and they got good grades. Nothing was done about it.

Participants also discussed additional strategies such as job opportunities, structure and discipline, and other strong role models that may be used by Black families to help them in their adaptive capacities so they might develop, grow, and reproduce.

Efforts are underway to develop an illustrated magazine of these Florida elders speaking to youth for classroom use in the public schools. This magazine will include work with an artist, an English professor, a journalist, a school counselor, and a teacher. Another project under consideration is a mass publication that would make the histories available to a larger public. In addition, the tapes will be preserved as archives—for use at other major universities.

DISCUSSION

This oral history research was undertaken to identify variables that might contribute to an understanding of Black family life in Tampa from the turn of the century to the present. Its focus was also to identify systems that Black families used within the community, to develop knowledge of families' survival techniques, to identify strategies that could be used as models for building leadership potential for Black youth, and finally, to leave a legacy to the Black youth of the next century. These oral histories represent a beginning, with the hope that others will be motivated to add to this knowledge.

These objectives were designed to learn participants' perceptions of restraining forces in their environment and their adaptive strategies. The resulting information was then added to the knowledge base, with material synthesized into theoretical concepts and hypotheses for future research. Also identified were variables that might be used by Black youth to reach a goodness of fit with their environment and preserve the history of Black family life.

Participants identified many restraining forces such as powerlessness, isolation, the political system, welfare systems, values, capitalism, lack of role models in economic and business settings, and several others. Adaptive supports they distinguished included strong family networks, use of a second language, strong role models (i.e., teachers and parents), church, strong values, work orientation, and many others. Supports and strategies that might benefit Black youth include strong role models, education, a strong economic orientation, discipline, joining together, and teachers and others who care.

Participants had many thoughts about how to leave a legacy to youth. They felt that they were moving in the right direction by sharing this information. They discussed the idea of a museum to store Black art and history that many of them possess, making these a part of the Black heritage that will live forever. In 1989, the art museum became a reality. The narratives of the Black elders help preserve the history of the Black experience in Tampa, contribute to the understanding of the meaning Black families give to their lives, identify the systems Black families used within the community, develop knowledge of Black family motivational and survival techniques, identify role models, and paint blueprints for building leadership for Black youth. It is hoped that Black youth of the next century will be able to read and understand a rich part of their heritage. The oral narratives can also be used in community centers and centers of Black excellence, in public schools, and in programs of social work education to develop cultural awareness and sensitivity.

REFERENCES

Billingsley, A. (1987). Black families in a changing society. In J. Dewart (Ed.), *The state of Black America* (pp. 99-103). New York: National Urban League.
Billingsley, A. (1992). *Climbing Jacob's ladder: The enduring legacy of African American families.* New York: Simon & Schuster.
Hartman, A. (1978). Diagrammatic assessment of family relationships. *Social Casework, 59,* 465-476.

Lewis, O. (1963). *The children of Sanchez: Autobiography of a Mexican family.* New York: Random House.

Martin, R. R. (1987). Oral history in social work education: Chronicling the Black experience. *Journal of Social Work Education, 23*(3), 5-10.

Martin, R. R. (1988). Black family adaptation, survival and growth strategies: An oral history research project. In A. Rodgers (Ed.), *Black family at the crossroads of development* (pp. 80-113). Columbia: University of South Carolina, College of Social Work.

Moynihan, D. (1965). The Negro family: The case for national action: A transaction social science and public policy report. In L. Rainwater & W. L. Yancey (Eds.), *The Moynihan report and the politics of controversy* (pp. 39-125). Cambridge: MIT Press.

7

THE REALITIES OF
SOVIET JEWISH MIGRATION
Illustrated Through Slava's Narratives

SELECTION OF TOPIC

I was interested in exploring the migration experiences of a group that
came to the United States to seek freedom. As my own group, African
Americans, were brought here in violation of their freedom, I was interested in how another people coped with leaving a homeland and adapting
to a new culture. I wanted to look at the experiences of recent immigrants
to capture the story "as it was happening." I assumed that political,
economic, and social forces motivated leaving and would also require
major adjustments once the immigrants were in the United States.

For social work researchers and practitioners in particular, the following interview with Slava suggests some of the work that can be done to
help facilitate settlement of immigrants to the United States. Immigrants
can be interviewed about the immigration process, assistance programs
they used, and other needs.

The story of American history is the story of immigrants. A great many
have come from distant shores, most in search of freedom of opportunity
and religion. Many have sought to start anew. One of the more recent
immigrant groups is composed of Soviet Jewish émigrés who began

AUTHOR'S NOTE: The narrative excerpts included in this chapter are from an interview
conducted July 12, 1990, at the YMCA in New York City, as part of my oral history research
project on Soviet Jewish migration.

arriving in the United States in the early 1970s and in much larger numbers toward the late 1980s.

In 1979, more than 20,000 Russian Jews sought refuge in America, matching the total number allowed to leave the Soviet Union and to enter the United States since the end of World War II. By 1981, the Soviet Union again tightened its borders, permitting only a trickle of Jews to leave. By 1984, only 254 Soviet Jews were permitted to travel west. This all changed by 1989. *Glasnost,* Soviet's new openness of official policy, had taken hold, and by 1991, the Soviet Union as a nation had collapsed. By now, 40,000 former Soviet Jews were being permitted into the United States and given refugee status; others came under a family reunification program. In addition to Jews, the United States has opened its borders to increasing numbers of immigrants from other areas of Eastern and Latin countries.

It is critically important for social work educators to understand adaptive and coping patterns of Soviet Jews and other new arrivals to more effectively learn from and serve them. Use of the oral history narrative allows the narrators to reconstruct and interpret their past, thereby giving continuity and meaning to their world, past and present, and in so doing, helping the helper understand their current experience and the meanings of that experience.

RESEARCH DESIGN AND
USE OF THE LITERATURE

Using the multidimensional perspective discussed in Chapter 2, I gathered oral histories from two middle-class Soviet émigrés who shared their experiences of what happened to them as a result of these transitions. Certain themes began to emerge as I analyzed the narratives using a stage of migration framework (Drachman & Shen-Ryan, 1991). I found that participants saw their lives as organized into two stages: (a) premigration and departure and (b) resettlement. This is consonant with Drachman and Shen-Ryan's groundbreaking work on a conceptual framework for understanding the migration process.

Drachman and Shen-Ryan (1991) write that "the stage framework has both generic and specific utility use." It can be applied to the individual immigrant because it offers "a lens for assessment of the individual in the particular circumstance of migration," and it "enables workers and service organizations to consider and address the experiences and needs of the new arrivals as well as of future newcomers." In so doing, it "enables service providers to examine the relevance of previous immigrant group experiences and the attendant service delivery patterns to present-day experiences and present program responses" (p. 629).

GETTING STARTED

When I began the search for participants to interview, I set up a meeting with the director of a program for émigrés and explained why I was conducting oral history research on Russian émigrés. The director did not understand how this piece of research would compare in any way with the research I had done previously with African Americans because "all of these émigrés were college educated." I thought his assumptions were interesting—that oral history was for uneducated groups. I was interested not in comparing the groups, however, but in the unique experiences of each. Oral history research begins with the assumption that everybody has stories to tell, that these stories are significant to the teller and the receiver, and that the stories of the participant are told in a comfortable language and through the narrator's cultural lens. This is what I learned from the émigrés. I will now present one interviewee's narratives and comment on some aspects of them in data analysis. The interviewee is Slava, a 24-year-old recent émigré living in New York City.

PREMIGRATION STAGE

Drachman and Shen-Ryan (1991) describe the long wait that the Soviet émigrés experienced before they were able to leave their country. Soviet officialdom viewed emigration as betrayal of one's country and of Soviet ideology. In the narrative below, Slava presents one man's experience.

OPPRESSION

My parents could not leave. I was trying to leave the Soviet Union so I worked for half a year after the graduation. The only possibility to leave it officially is to get the invitation from Israel. Someone invited me to Israel to join their family or relatives. This invitation was received only by me not my parents. My parents tried to leave Leningrad 15 years ago when the whole emigration began, but were unable to get an invitation for a lot of years. Someone in Israel had sent a lot of invitations to them but, it was known by 100% that the KGB took them away, intercepted the mail. So they never received an invitation before I received mine. And when I was in the application process for emigration they finally received their invitation. I and my brother received it. But due to several circumstances, they couldn't apply immediately, so I left alone and first came to Vienna, Austria, and spent about 2 weeks there. Then I went to Rome in Italy and applied for refugee status of the U.S. Embassy in Rome.

And at that time, Jewish people who were emigrating from the Soviet Union had to apply for refugee status in the third country, which for me was Italy. We couldn't apply for the status in Moscow so the whole process was like this.

IMMIGRATION QUOTAS

And at this time, when I came in 1989 to Rome, there already existed a problem of so-called Soviet refuseniks. They were refused an entrance visa to the United States because of quotas which existed in American policy for refugees. So my application was denied, and I had to stay in Italy and I knew nothing about my fate and future.

I waited a couple of months and I decided to reapply. Why I decided this but not to go to Israel? Well, in Israel I have nobody, no friends, no relatives, and this invitation was the only possibility to leave Russia. In the States I have a lot of friends who immigrated 1 or 2 years ago before me, and there were a lot of other friends of my parents who immigrated maybe 15 years ago, 10 years ago. The majority of them is from the musical sphere because my father is a musician. He plays viola, at Kirov Ball in Leningrad and the main theater of opera and ballet in Leningrad. He was on tour in the States in the 1970s with Leningrad Philharmonic Orchestra and many, many countries during a period since 1965, even before I was born.

RELIGIOUS FREEDOM

We had only one synagogue in Leningrad. Usually nearly all Jewish people came to this synagogue on Jewish holidays and because of that fact the synagogue was the only one in the big city. The place was overcrowded every time and they stopped traffic and there was a lot of police. But it was very dangerous to visit there 'cause KGB was always there checking. Every college, every university in Russia has so-called "first department" which means that there is a KGB office. They invited me to this first department, and they showed my pictures from the synagogue. And they told me that I had only one choice. That meant I can go to synagogue but I have to leave the Young Communist League, a member of which I was, and as a result of this to leave the citizenship.

OPPORTUNITIES FOR THE PRIVILEGED CLASS

My father never joined the Communist party but he still worked as a cellist in the orchestra. He was the head of the violas' group in this orchestra, but they had no other choice because the majority of musicians in Leningrad are Jewish. They didn't want to join Communist party, but if not them, who will play? So, he played in this orchestra and he went abroad and was so-called privileged class of those people who had an opportunity to go abroad once a year.

THE NEED TO STRETCH THE DOLLAR

His salary in this tour was about $100 a day, but Soviet officials took away about 80% so he had only $20 a day. Right now, still, every Soviet orchestra which comes on tour here or somewhere else, they bring in luggage a lot of dry soups, meat and cans and so on and so forth. They have to cook meals at their hotel in order to save money to buy something for their families in Russia. But still, I had an opportunity to get some clothes from abroad brought from States in Europe, and electronic equipment like tape recorders, a VCR, and a TV.

THE OPPRESSION OF JEWS

During my studies at school I understood how everything was tied with young Communist party leaders, which I had to attend and which I hated, but without it I did not have an opportunity to graduate from high school because of being Jewish. I didn't have an opportunity to be accepted at the Institute and this meant that I have to go to armed forces to serve for 2 years. When I was at the age of 18, there, it is the age when you must go to the Soviet army if you are not in the Institute.

And, I was really afraid that I could go to Afghanistan and be killed there because even some of my friends were on this war; some were injured, some were killed. So, I tried to go to the Institute in the so-called military department. Here I studied military sciences, and besides the sciences were finally connected with my own profession. I could join the Military Institute as this was available.

When I graduated I became an officer of the Soviet Army, and when I immigrated I had to put on the table that I was an officer in an army department. My document said that I'm a officer of the Soviet Army and this was really, very difficult 10 years ago. A lot of people were denied an exit visa because of that fact.

Leningrad was one of the biggest centers of anti-Semitic organizations in the Soviet Union. There are few Jews in Ukraine or in small towns of somewhere else in Russia, because they left many, many years ago in the beginning of the 20th century.

And besides all of them who didn't leave, they went to big cities as Moscow, Leningrad, Kiev in Ukraine. So, the city of Leningrad was the largest center of Jewish people. And, a lot of anti-Semitic groups were there.

The name of them is called Pamyat which is famous all over the world now because of such magazines as Newsweek, which published about this radical group. They had open meetings in Leningrad in parks, and everywhere, even the road, new slogans like, "Leningrad is the city for Russians."

And [they say] Jews are in charge of the government, and the fault of Jews is that they made a revolution in 1917 and that a Czar was shot and his family was shot; that the main people who played the leading rulers in this revolution along with Lenin were Jewish. And they blame all Jews [for] troubles that all peoples of the Soviet Union had in these 70 years.

And besides it's true that the writers' union in the Soviet Union has about maybe 60 or 70% Jewish writers, and the literature in the Soviet Union plays much bigger role than in the United States or somewhere in Europe. Because maybe people don't have an opportunity to buy food or clothes, so they want to read more, as well as cinema, by the way. These anti-Semitic groups wanted a purer Russian culture. They wanted pure Russian literature, Russian music and so on. So they wanted all Jewish people to leave these units as writers, cinema units and so on. And they reached their goal because in this year they managed to separate the writers' union into the union of Russian writers and union of Jewish writers.

MY CHANCE TO GO

The situation with the immigration was much easier than 10 or 15 years ago. The application process was easier and a lot of people wanted to leave because of that. And I decided that I must do it [leave] immediately—because the situation in the Soviet Union was really unpredictable. And nobody knew how long Gorbachev will be in Kremlin—and nobody knew how long maybe army will take power in their hands. And what does it mean to Jewish people and what does it mean to Russian people? And a lot of people wanted to go because of the fear, and I managed to receive an invitation from Israel It was very hard because a lot of people tried to write to Israel to their friends' relatives. They wrote their names, their date of birth, and their address, which was necessary to make an invitation for them. But a lot of these letters disappeared.

Through this narrative, Slava has described the premigration phase of this emigration to the United States. He identified and described the oppressive forces that he and his compatriots experienced in Russia. The oppressive forces permeated every phase of their lives. They endured religious prosecution, job refusals, scarcity of food, anti-Semitic groups, persecution for the Russian revolution, and the final insult of the anti-Semitic organization: "Jews, leave our country, leave our culture, leave our units." The Jews found different ways of coping, which included nonattendance at the synagogue, traveling to the outskirts of the large cities to seek food, changing their names, and waiting for the opportunity to emigrate.

THE RESETTLEMENT

The second part of the oral history interview is discussed under the second stage of migration framework. Slava begins to weave his narrative about resettlement by describing why he chose to come to New York and how people move where their social supports are.

If a person wants to go to a city like Los Angeles, or San Francisco or somewhere else, he must have a so-called grant from his relatives or his friends. They pay some amount to their Jewish community and this community receives new immigrants. But New York is open for those who have no such grant. Besides I had a lot of friends only in New York City.

SERVICES IN PLACE

So, I came here and a friend of mine, he met me at JFK and I went to Brooklyn—where his relatives live. So I spent about 2 weeks with them in their apartment. Then during the week I wanted to find an apartment for myself. So by chance, I met a friend of mine with whom we were in Italy. And here I met him in the office of an agency for all those who come to New York City. It's New York Association for New Americans. He told me that he is living at the 92nd St. Y, and there is a lot of facilities and there are cheaper rooms and there is a special program which is called "Passage to Freedom." I came here, I had an interview with the director of this residence, and I was accepted here for residence, this program, Passage to Freedom.

We have a discount in rent, but we have to live with a roommate so we share a room—and also we share a kitchen and a bathroom with all residents on the floor. And [pause] that's the story of my coming to the 92nd St.

Here Slava is talking about his concern and his worry about those who are left behind.

There are [currently] a lot of anti-Semitic people within my parents' neighborhood. And besides, there were a lot of Jewish people who left this neighborhood and there are a lot of Russians who are waiting for new apartments. So they want to force everybody to leave. And [since I've left] my parents have received a lot of threatening letters from these groups with the content that says: "Go away from here. Go to your son, you have no choice," and so on.

A friend of my family said that my parents were put into their so-called blacklist of this organization called Pamyat and that means that they could be persecuted or killed or something like this. And the police do nothing to stop this violence and so the officials do nothing to stop that. So, the situation is indeed very dangerous. And my brother, he cannot do anything alone to protect my parents.

THE OPPORTUNITIES

I wanted to change my profession when I came here—partly because of that fact that I had no choice to select a university or institute that I wanted [in Leningrad]. I liked my profession, I'm an engineer, but I wanted to start a business and there are no business schools in the Soviet Union at all.

You cannot apply your education in the Leningrad life. 'Cause there is no free market in the Soviet Union [at the time of his experience]. The economics is different and you cannot start a business. My diploma, which I got there in the Soviet Union, is an equivalent of their bachelor's degree.

I wanted to apply to the business school for master's degree. I wanted to apply to top schools as Harvard, Yale, Columbia, N.Y.U., Wharton School of Business, or University of Chicago. But in order to do that I have to take a test of English as a foreign language and Graduate Management Admissions Test (GMAT). And in order to be accepted at such schools, I have to get a score of about 620, top 10% of all those who took this exam. I have already taken both of them. And this score which I received is 550; it's much lower than it should be. I can take again and I'll do it. But the main difficulty is, and that is the differences between cultures and between the education. In the Soviet education there are no examinations with answer sheets like multiple choice answers. And you never mark the answer sheet with a pencil and you never choose between four or five answers, one correct answer or the best answer. All examinations are like the table, two chairs and you are professor and I'm a student, and orally, or you write something. But it is never machine scores. So it was the first examination of such kind that was really different to me because it was timed and the first examination of such kind is always difficult.

Right now, the goal is to find a job and to have an experience of American fulltime jobs and maybe if company will be interested in my education later, they will help me with my graduate studies. If not, I'll apply to the graduate school by myself without any help. And that's it. Right now, I'm taking a course in typing and word processing in the school. The education is paid by New York Association for New Americans—so it's free for me. And it takes about 12 to 16 weeks to complete this course. And I have already completed 3 weeks and I can type about 20 or 25 gross words a minute already—and, the word processing, I believe that it will be very helpful in every kind of job and in every kind of studies here.

CONCLUSION

Slava's narrative highlights some of the special challenges involved with interviewing and editing oral histories of people for whom English is not a first language. Greater patience and listening ability is required of interviewees. For the editing of this piece, I received help from people familiar with the syntax of Russian-born speakers of English, as well as historical and cultural details about which I was not fully acquainted. Most Americans would be stumped by some of Slava's references without careful editing on the researcher's part. Slava's narrative is similar to others in which people referred to historical events, the details and accuracy of which must be checked and verified by the oral historian.

Although Slava's narrative is only one person's experience, it provides insight about his homeland; about the premigration forces of political, economic, and social oppression; and about the coping and adaptive ways in which he has adjusted to a different culture. Putting the total interview in the context of the many interviews that I and others have done allows me to make generalizations about the findings.

REFERENCE

Drachman, D., & Shen-Ryan, A. (1991). Immigrants and refugees. In A. Gitterman (Ed.), *Handbook of social work practice with vulnerable populations* (pp. 618-646). New York: Columbia University Press.

8

RECAPTURING THE PURPOSE OF
SETTLEMENTS THROUGH ORAL HISTORY

THE ORAL HISTORY PROJECT

SELECTION OF TOPIC

Oral history can be used to obtain and analyze the history of movements and institutions as well as individuals and groups of people. Dr. Ivor Echols, a colleague at the University of Connecticut, and I were particularly interested in the settlement movement of the late 19th century and the role of African Americans in that movement (see Martin & Echols, 1989). Well into the 20th century, social services were delivered on a separate basis because of socially acceptable and institutionalized racism and segregation. Settlement houses served particular neighborhoods. Because Blacks were usually segregated, there was a need for separate settlement houses despite the egalitarian purposes of the movement. Thus, the plan to investigate settlement houses in Connecticut was formed.

LITERATURE REVIEW

The writings of several authorities (Axinn & Levin, 1982; Davis, 1984; Trattner, 1979) portray a vivid picture of the settlement (house) movement of the last quarter of the 19th and early 20th centuries. The purposes of

AUTHOR'S NOTE: A version of this chapter was presented with Dr. Ivor Echols to the Council on Social Work Education, March 4-9, 1989, in Chicago (see Martin & Echols, 1989). Narratives and data are from interviews conducted in 1988 with leaders involved in settlement houses and community centers in Connecticut.

settlement workers, according to Trattner, were to "bridge the gap between the classes and races, eliminate the sources of distress . . . improve urban living and working conditions. . . . Theirs was the preventive approach" (p. 134).

Unfair labor practices, child labor, lack of educational opportunities for poor people, overcrowding, and poor housing resulting in "scarcely endurable" sanitary conditions were some of the most serious social problems of the day. It was these conditions that settlement house workers sought to improve through community involvement, dialogue, and social and economic reform, whereas the Charity Organization Society, the other developing social service system, had emphasized the "individual and moral causes of destitution" (Trattner, 1979, p. 136). To the settlers, who actually moved into the settlement house and became part of the community, "poverty resulted from the denial of opportunity, and pressure was exerted for legislative reform designed to affirm and expand an inherent core of human dignity" (Axinn & Levin, 1982, p. 6).

This reform agenda was established in dialogue with the neighborhood residents who also lived in and around the settlement house. The values, ideas, and efforts of those who became involved in the founding of the settlement movement may be summed up as follows: "The philosophy of the settlement house movement led to social and economic change—settlement house residents would say 'Do, do' " (Trattner, 1979, pp. 136-137). Davis (1984) describes the settlement workers' roles as promoting justice, efficiency, and order in living. He stresses the settlers'

> religious zeal with which to create a better world . . . campaigns against child labor and prostitution . . . better housing and women's rights . . . [and] the rhetoric of the progressives that stressed truth, justice, democracy, and the faith that it was possible to build a better world. (p. xx)

RESEARCH PURPOSE

This chapter reports on an oral history research project with founders and pioneers in the settlement movement who believed that they could change some of the problems of the world by centering their activities in the neighborhood-based settlement houses. Although much of the literature regarding settlement houses focuses on large cities, such as Chicago, New York, and Boston, this is a story told by men and women of Connecticut regarding the legacy of settlements in Connecticut. The chapter is an attempt to share some of the needs, ideas, and efforts of those who became involved with the settlement houses; to document the roles of African Americans in settlements and in neighborhood center work (a

20th-century outgrowth of the settlement movement); and to revive the philosophy of settlements for today's practitioners.

PARTICIPANTS AND SETTING

The research participants who shared oral histories presented in this chapter are Ms. Joyce Griffin, Black, executive director of Yerwood Center, who describes the history of Yerwood Community Center, a settlement started by an African American woman; Mabel C. Donnelly, Ph.D., White, longtime board member, Hartford Neighborhood Centers; Mr. Ewell Newman, White, retired executive director of Hull House; and Mr. George Pipkin, Black, executive director of Hull House at the time of these interviews. The three institutions involved are Hull House, a settlement house founded in Bridgeport at the peak of the settlement movement in 1886; Hartford Neighborhood Centers—one of the earliest programs of this amalgam was Hartford Settlement, founded in 1894; and Yerwood Center, a neighborhood house founded by Dr. Joyce Yerwood in 1943.

Again, the number of participants is small. By putting the total in the context of the many interviews that I have done, however, I make generalizations about the findings.

THE NARRATIVES

YERWOOD CENTER: BEGINNINGS

Ms. Griffin reported that in 1933, Dr. Joyce Yerwood earned an M.D. at Meharry Medical College and in 1935 moved to Stamford, Connecticut. Dr. Yerwood began inviting neighborhood youth to use her backyard as a gathering place. From those informal beginnings in 1937 grew the formation of a chorus—which produced an operetta as a fund-raiser for a local church. By 1939, she had created the Negro Little Theater in a store on West Broad Street. In 1943, the Negro Community Center was formed. In 1948, she purchased a vacant store on West Main Street, which became the West Main Street Community Center and later the Yerwood Center. The Yerwood Center moved to its present location in 1975. The community responded with funds to build the new center on Fairfield Avenue on the site of what had been Stevens School. Ms. Griffin supported her discussion with newspaper articles in a supplement to the *Stamford Advocate* (see Reilly, 1975). Ms. Griffin said of Dr. Yerwood:

> Her father was a country doctor as well, and her mother, a schoolteacher, died when the young ladies were quite young. So they were raised actually

by their father and, I believe, an aunt that she used to speak of. And the choice was being a doctor or being an actress, and I think somebody decided, the father probably decided that being a doctor was the lesser of the two evils. But he didn't get just one, he got two and I think Dr. Connie was more into research and health, whereas Dr. Joyce Yerwood became a medical practitioner.

We are all very well aware of the struggle that Dr. Yerwood had in getting the place up here on the hill and it was honestly and truly her heart. And she worked day and night. I would get a call from her saying "Girl, (she still had this Texas accent) where have you been?"

HULL HOUSE: BEGINNINGS

Mr. Newman became executive director of the Hull Neighborhood House in 1949. During the early 1930s, he had been a resident of Hull House, the most well-known settlement, founded by Jane Addams in Chicago in 1886. Mr. Pipkin has been the executive director of the Hull Neighborhood Centers since 1968. Prior to coming to Bridgeport, he worked for the Cleveland Neighborhood Centers. He and Mr. Newman complimented each other on their ability to recall the development and progress of the Hull Neighborhood Center.

Hull House began as the Associated Charities for Industrial Relief in 1886. In 1920, there were four centers: Franklin Day Nursery; the Main Street Day Nursery; Paul Bright; and Hull Neighborhood House. All functioned under one board. In 1949, the name still was Associated Charities for Industrial Relief: Hull Home Settlement, New England Federation of Settlements. In 1988, Hull Neighborhood House, Inc., celebrated 102 years of progress.

HARTFORD NEIGHBORHOOD
CENTERS: BEGINNINGS

Dr. Donnelly, longtime board member (during the 1960s and early 1970s) of Hartford Neighborhood Centers, researched and published *A Century of Service: Hartford Neighborhood Centers 1872-1972* (1972). She tells about the early Hartford Neighborhood Centers, a merger of six formerly autonomous programs: Union for Home Work, 1872-1939; Hartford Settlement, 1894-1939; College Settlement Association (Spruce Street Settlement, 1907-1926, and Mitchell House, 1927-1960); North End Community Center, 1931-1956; and Union Settlement, 1939-1956. These merged into Hartford Neighborhood Centers, 1956 to the present. Dr. Donnelly relates,

Well, the Union for Home Work was founded in 1872. It is the oldest ancestor of Hartford Neighborhood Centers which continues today in Hartford. The founders of the Union were a small group of women who met privately and who had given aid, bandage rolling and that sort of thing during the Civil War and they were concerned about the plight of the immigrant poor of whom there were many.

Dr. Donnelly gives some background information on the founders of the settlement movement in Hartford. Below she raises the question and fills in the answer for my enlightenment.

Now, where does Mrs. Elizabeth Sluyter and her spouse Steven come in? They came in because, obviously, with a good place you have to have good staff, and also with their strong Protestant connections obviously.

Mrs. Sluyter, whose husband was a retired Civil War Captain, was very active in the beginning of the Union for Home Work located on the site that is now Constitution Plaza in Hartford, Connecticut. Thirty percent of the people of Hartford were foreign-born. She wrote an article on "How to Provide Good Family Dinners for 15 cents" in order to share information with families who were working for 5 cents an hour.

One of her daughters, a Mrs. Ayers, hosted a meeting which was called the Social Workers Club of Hartford. The Union of Home Work joined the Hartford Social Settlement. With help from the Hartford Seminary, the organization raised money to get building for housing for the poor. Jane Addams came to Hartford in 1903 to visit the program.

This type of invaluable historic information may or may not be well documented in written records. Often it is lost in dusty archives. In cases in which some of the information is documented, I have credited them in the references. The subjective experiences of the participants as expressed in the interviews are new, however, and can be integrated into the current body of knowledge. It is important to ensure that the history of the settlement movement and the social work profession be preserved, highlighted, and made available to today's students and practitioners.

PROBLEMS ADDRESSED BY SETTLEMENTS

RACIAL PROBLEMS

Of the three centers discussed in this chapter, Yerwood was the latest to be organized. It was founded at a time when race relations were particularly conflictual. As Ms. Griffin relates,

One of the reasons why the doctor chose to work with the Black children in the community, years ago, was because there wasn't any place in Stamford for young people to get together socially. People don't like to think of it as such. You attended the same school as the Whites, but you were discriminated against economically in that you . . . they managed to keep you out of places they didn't want you to go, because you couldn't afford to go. You could very well live up in the Ridges if you could *afford* to live up in the Ridges, but not many of them could, so, I mean that certainly was no concern of theirs. You know.

The racial divisions actually would show even more when you left the elementary school area for the junior high school area and then went to high school. That's when the line would definitely be drawn as to whether you are Black or White. So that's where the exclusion began. We still have a lot of racism, economic racism.

When Dr. Yerwood stopped practicing medicine, she kept her license so that she could work down at Liberation House. I know that she has seen it all from one generation to another.

I came to the center as a child. As a matter of fact, so did my secretary. I'll have her come in and talk. My uncle who is now 75 years old (I'll run and get some pictures) was a part of this community center. And Dr. Yerwood and her sister, Connie, were instrumental in sending an awful lot of children out of this area to college. They are now in their 60s and 70s. My aunt, in particular, who passed away a year ago, went to school in Texas and she lived with Dr. Connie. Dr. Yerwood would send the young ladies where her sister was so that you would have someone, some type of supervision and chaperoning. There are 22 years between my brother and myself, he was young at that particular time and he is now 65. So you can see the long contact she has had with these people from the time they were children. Right up to the point where they became adults with grandchildren. And even at my brother's age, she would call him up and say, "Clarence, get up here and fix my car." It was just something that when she called, you did. The thought of hesitating just never crossed your mind.

Ms. Griffin presented, for perusal, photos of Dr. Yerwood at the dedication of the Negro Community Center in 1943, as well as current photos and many old and new newspaper clippings (e.g., Eliopoulos, 1987).

Dr. Yerwood always said a child changed her life: When she told a group of children that she was ready to start her medical practice, one child said to her, "You're a colored doctor. I never knew that a colored woman could be a doctor."

She said that statement changed what she would do for the rest of her life. She wanted to give Black people and children in the community opportunities to learn how much they could accomplish in their own lives. She worked and served as teacher and role model for generations of Stamford children. She was the first Black woman physician in Fairfield County, Connecticut. (see also Reilly, 1987)

WOMEN'S RIGHTS

Dr. Donnelly related how she became interested in neighborhood centers after being inspired by woman's suffragist Isabella Beecher Hooker, sister of Harriet Beecher Stowe. She also was inspired by reading Riis's (1890) book, *How the Other Half Lives,* and was well into "benevolent amateurism" when she became a board member of Hartford Neighborhood Centers in the 1960s.

HULL HOUSE AND THE SETTLEMENT'S MANDATES

In the narratives below, Mr. Newman discusses Hull House and its programs in relation to the settlement movement.

Ah, well, some of the same needs arose, the same problems arose. There on the west side of Chicago and developing here in Bridgeport—may be a few years difference, and one of the interesting phenomena about it. The early part of the 20th century, the Black population was still concentrated in the rural South. The problems of assimilation and adaptation to American culture, that was the pride and motivation of the settlement. Concern and the exploitation of child labor. The leader, nationwide against child labor, the movement to get legislation to protect children and women came out of Hull House in Chicago. She was Florence Kelley, one of Miss Addams' close associates and staff people. They pioneered in that movement.

There was another dimension of this which had a great deal of value and yet sometimes the icing on the cake kind of thing, and even back to London, to Canon Barnett and the first settlement houses there. So many families lived in such poverty, so crowded together, and such little opportunity to cultivate themselves culturally. They recognized the need to provide people with training and experiences where they could develop appreciation for the arts, music, sculpture, domestic skills, sewing, crocheting. The result, for example, Hull House in Chicago became the best art school in the entire city, if not the only art school.

She was still there when I was there and I took classes with her, Miss Enella Benedict. They had classes in sculpturing, in pottery making and in weaving, and in dancing, ballet, folk, in literature, in writing and in the classics. Remember Benny Goodman? Benny Goodman got his training in the clarinet at Hull House. This was all the cultural part of it, but it was important to the people at the time. It helped them get out of the loneliness and the poverty in which they grew up.

HULL HOUSE PROGRAM

Ah, we had an evening program for teenagers, recreation groups of course, discussions, and various problems. There was a mothers' club and there were some sewing classes, but we did not get into the problems of depth that George is today. We didn't have the money, as a matter of fact we had to rely . . . we had an endowment fund. It's comfortable, but it's not gigantic is it?

But even in those days the Community Chest or United Way never raised more than a million or half million a year and our budget in the 19 years I was there I think our annual budget never exceeded 80 or 85 thousand dollars. Am I right? The bulk of this came from Community Chest or United Way. It was a small amount that came out of endowment. Then we charged the nursery fees. The average weekly fee that we collected was about $3.50 or something like that.

HARTFORD NEIGHBORHOOD CENTERS

Dr. Donnelly continues by describing the services provided by the Hartford Neighborhood Centers:

Women gathered monies together and provided a coffee house for the poor so they could get at least one hot meal a day free if the people were truly poor, as vouched for, by the way, by local ministers. They had a problem in those days about the undeserving poor and they were very strict about that. They also provided reading rooms for, ah, young boys and particularly newspaper sellers and anyone else who was willing to read. Many of the boys obviously took advantage of this opportunity. The building was on Market Street.

They offered skills—this is very interesting—skills, school training, and day care. Day care was 5 cents a day per child, starting with breakfast early in the morning and going on until the mothers got home from work and since their work was typically an entire day, the children got fed.

About the skills—sewing machines were there, cooking skills, laundry skills, because these were the jobs that immigrant women took when they were available. On weekends they took children and adults into what was then the country, West Hartford. On the trolley to the limits of what was then a 5-cent fare.

At the beginning, the Union had only 190 paid members. There was no board of directors until many years after the founding. The decisions were made by officers and standing committees.

YERWOOD CENTER

Ms. Griffin explains the cultural benefits provided by the Yerwood Center:

She [Dr. Yerwood] was heavily into recreation, cultural things, like this is a play she had put on in 1949, and she had a Yerwood chorus. The Yerwood women, a group that was formed, the Yerwood chorus, men's chorus, the Yerwood chorale, and she had new plays and she had her cabarets, and you were continuously into plays—you were given the cultural aspects with changes. I mean you were a group of Black youth putting on plays about Japanese with customs and music. So she didn't discriminate with respect to you or by just having to learn about your own.

COMPARING EARLY
MISSION WITH TODAY'S MISSION

In the following narratives, the narrators are responding to the question of whether neighborhood centers today are promoting social justice that is based on the settlement philosophy. Mr. Pipkin begins,

As Ewell has indicated, I came at a very prosperous time [the year 1968], in terms of federal intervention and government funding. But it's interesting that some of the same things that Ewell had talked about are some of the things that we are providing in a kind of more technology as shown even in the human service area, where we had the Golden Age Club that Ewell talked about, and the day care centers. The old came out just like the youngsters to our building.

We have senior citizens day care for the same old people who cannot stay at home by themselves and we have day care for youngsters. We have a new therapeutic day care program, services for at-risk children, our first in a program funded only to serve six children and six families, and an adoption and foster care service [for] adoptive families. Also the center provides child development programs [such as] Head Start, minority male image programs, tutorial programs, karate programs, a girls' residential home, support networks, Roberto Clemente condominiums, and Bridgeport Montessori program.

Dr. Donnelly adds,

Well, certainly day care is at the top of everybody's list. Additional programs are work with senior citizens, job training, youth groups, and tenants' organizations.

Ms. Griffin continues,

> Among the programs we provide are arts and crafts, counseling services, summer day camp, gym programs, a teen parent program, a senior center in the evenings, and a Correctional Parole Pilot Program Center. We intend to center a lot of the programs we are writing now around the pool. We just entered into a martial arts club. We intend to rehab the floor lighting, stage, bathroom facilities, have the gymnasium reconverted so that we can capture some of the Black organizations' business.
>
> We are told that one organization paid $17,000 recently for the use of a hall in another area. Of course we would never have charged that amount of money. Where they won't have to beg quite so much from the funding agencies, whereby when ever we ask, if they say no, we say, oh so what? If you don't want to give us the $10,000 we will raise it some other way, but instead of having to go and beg to them for 60, 70, 80, 100 thousand dollars. That's a lot of begging. Because when we need to run the center, we need approximately $450,000.

HAVE THEY MADE A
DIFFERENCE: BUILT A BETTER WORLD?

In this section, the narrators talk about the difference the centers have made. Dr. Donnelly begins,

> I do think that. I think anybody who has ever been over to the center—and seen the children with low cerebral activity, you realize, what else would they be doing? Would they be at home sitting in front of a TV set?
>
> During the early period, the workers were more Darwinian in approach, (survival of the fittest) but the emphasis was still on giving a chance to the hardest hit. In 1914 the settlement still had a budget of less than $4,000 a year. There was a conversion of working with a certain kind of client to another kind of client—the soup kitchens to the homeless. The work of neighborhood people was assisted by the educated people.

Dr. Donnelly describes how the Hartford Neighborhood Centers grew out of a need for assimilation of immigrants, overcrowded conditions, hungry stomachs, hungry minds, homelessness, lack of skills, day care, and poor economics. Only the groups have changed. Day care, housing, home-lessness, lack of skills, and abuse and neglect are pressing issues of today as well.

Discrimination was a problem when the Yerwood Center opened. Ms. Griffin notes that today there are still serious problems of discrimination and race relations. Black students are still searching for their identity, and recreation is still an essential service provided. Ms. Griffin relates,

> Yes, the neighborhood centers have made a difference because there are still some very, very nice children out there, still some very nice children (I'm calling them children because I am 43) whose goal is to have some nice neat fun and this is the place for them to come. Parents don't have to worry about them because they know they will be supervised. It also is good for the children because during certain periods of their lives they are able to be with their own kind, giving them a feeling of belonging. It has helped the Black community also with the fact that they have moved up out of this area.

> To me, once you remove an educational institution from a community is an indication that you have given up on that particular . . . and the Blacks in their struggle for equality . . . pushing busing, destroyed their community. [Yerwood Center is now located on the grounds of the elementary school which she attended. And in fact, the gymnasium in use is a part of the old school.]

In the narrative below, Mr. Newman expresses his belief that settlements served as a springboard for many youth.

> I think we played a much stronger role than maybe we are given credit for. Lot of young women and young men learned how to play the trombone, they learned ballet dancing, and so on. They carried the philosophy of the settlements and went on to greater things.

In the following narrative, Mr. Pipkin describes some of the late 19th- and 20th-century problems. He also discusses how many of the problems persist today. New technology and different groups served, however, have demanded change in the way the services are provided.

> I think also, and I agree with Ewell entirely, the leadership roles, the role of developing leadership has had implications for so many of our people have come from, if Jessie wants to use the term, grass roots, and just gone right up through the settlement movement and moved right out into other areas, and carried that influence, that settlement philosophy influence, that impact into other areas, and we really are not given credit for it.

> There were many problems of the late 19th and early 20th century such as assimilation, adaptation to America, loss of self-esteem, poverty, women's day care needs, and children's issues such as exploitation of child labor, economics, housing, homelessness, overcrowding, poverty, education, lack of skills and are as persistent today. Problems of assimilation

continue, only the majority of the groups represented are not Irish, Italian, Jewish, Greek. [They are] Hispanics, Asians and other new Americans such as Ethiopians, Afri-Caribbeans, Latins, and Cambodians. Other problems are day care needs, abuse and neglect, lack of skills, need for adoptive homes, housing/homelessness, economics, and race relations. The problems still exist as do many old services, however, the services are now provided more in line with new technology (technological changes such as computers, applied behavioral sciences with trained workers and the like).

CONCLUSION

This oral history project has helped to recapture the spirit of what settlements were about. Seen in the eyes and heard in the voices of the participants are not only the ideas, commitments, and values of the directors and board members but also the eagerness with which they continue the settlement movement in the present time. Graduate students of social work are also playing a vital role in providing services to the agencies. For example, one agency operates a therapeutic day care center and is involved with adoptive placements, which require well-trained social workers with knowledge about human development and life tasks and skills in interviewing, assessing, and intervention. There is a need for trained workers who understand diversity and the neighborhood as a unit, as well as normal and exceptional developmental struggles under conditions of poverty and aggression. This has implications for social work education: to address the issues and needs and provide more effective methods of providing services in times that are as difficult as those in which the settlement movement began. There is also a rapidly growing interest of the social work profession in the use of oral history to preserve professional history as well as individual history. Oral history can help those in the human services professions look at the pattern of delivery of services through time.

Oral histories such as these presented in this chapter can give organizations and board members an opportunity to recapture their history. This in turn can help newer committee members find their way and become excited about the work. They might then have hope that their own thoughts might be heard more widely and have implications for sound change. More than three decades ago, Gans (1964) considered the settlement's function in regard to its effectiveness in the War on Poverty. He saw settlements as dated and ineffective, noting that the settlement house was founded 100 years ago in America by an earlier generation who attempted to remove the deprivations of urban poverty. By Gans's scorecard, settlements were not doing very well: They did not know their clients, they imported social workers to provide programs to which the settlements were overcommitted, and they failed to recognize a new low-income population of changing race and ethnicity. They were being supplanted by community action agencies who truly represented their constituencies. Looking back, we know the significance of the War on Poverty has been written into history. Community action agencies have died a natural death or have metamorphosed into advocacy organizations. Meanwhile, the battles for social justice continue. Settlement houses (neighborhood centers) have continued to flex their muscles to address old needs expressed in ever changing forms. They have survived and, according to their storytellers—via the oral histories—have achieved much justification for the dreams of their founders.

REFERENCES

Axinn, J., & Levin, H. (1982). *Social welfare: A history of the American response to need* (2nd ed.). New York: Harper & Row.

Davis, A. F. (1984). *Spearheads for reform: The social settlements and the progressive movement.* New Brunswick, NJ: Rutgers University Press.

Donnelly, M. C. (1972). *A century of service: Hartford neighborhood centers 1872-1972.* Hartford, CT: Hartford Neighborhood Centers.

Eliopoulos, C. (1987, October 3). Center was doctor's gift to Stamford. *Stamford Advocate,* p. 1.

Gans, H. (1964). Redefining the settlement's function for the War on Poverty. *Social Work, 9*(4), 3-12.

Martin, R. R., & Echols, I. (1989, March). *Recapturing the purpose of settlements through the oral histories of pioneers.* Paper presented to the Council on Social Work Education, Chicago.

Reilly, P. (1975, May 4). Your invitation. *Stamford Advocate,* Suppl., pp. 1-8.

Reilly, P. (1987, October 3). Dr. Yerwood, civil leader, dies. *Stamford Advocate,* Suppl., p. 1.

Riis, J. (1890). *How the other half lives.* New York: Scribner.

Trattner, W. L. (1979). *From poor law to welfare state: A history of social welfare in America* (2nd ed.). New York: Free Press.

9

ORAL HISTORY METHODOLOGY TO EXAMINE ISSUES OF ADOLESCENT MOTHERS

RESEARCH PROBLEM

The purpose of this chapter is, first, to discuss the technique of examining African American family issues through the oral history methodology and, second, to illustrate this method with narratives of female African American adolescents as they discuss teenage pregnancy. In the first part of the chapter, attention is given to rationale for using this method for understanding African American family issues. The second part of the chapter presents the oral history narratives of adolescent mothers as they struggle for competence, autonomy and relatedness, identity, and self-direction.

LITERATURE REVIEW

According to Billingsley (1987), the African American family is struggling for stability. He lists several major trends that define the African American family. These changes are evident in the family structure, such as a decline of 25% in married-couple families since 1960. During that same period, single-headed families increased 22%. Some of the same

AUTHOR'S NOTE: This chapter is adapted from "Oral History Methodology: Examination of Issues Among Adolescent Mothers," by R. R. Martin, 1991, *Family Science Review,* 4(3), pp. 109-122. Used by permission. Names of the narrators and names mentioned in the narratives are pseudonyms.

issues concerning the African American family that were addressed by Moynihan in 1965 and were addressed by Billingsley in 1987 are said to be present today. These are rising levels of poverty, declining levels of income, rising levels of unemployment, declining levels of family stability, a rising underclass, and a struggling middle class. Also high on the list of changes, according to Billingsley, are the large increase in the African American high school student dropout rate, the large number of teenage pregnancies (a decrease of 9.9% but still a high 87 per 1,000), the increase in the number of African American men incarcerated, and the high proportion of African American men and women serving in the armed services, primarily at the enlisted rank.

Despite these negative statistics, an amazing number of African American families are stable. They have adapted, survived, prospered, and created opportunities for achievement of their young—often against severe odds. It often is said that a lesser people would not have survived (Martin, 1988). Adaptation, as used in this chapter, refers to the active efforts of African Americans "over their life span to reach a goodness-of-fit with their environment so that they may survive, develop, and achieve reproductive success" (Germain, 1979, p. 8).

Although researchers collect and analyze data on diverse populations, more thought should be given to the cultural perspective. When viewed closely through the cultural lens of the participants, strengths, adaptation, and coping are visible from a different perspective. A method that allows this is oral history: a method of communication that always has been an integral part of African American culture (Martin, 1987).

A rationale for using oral history methodology in researching African American families is that it provides a means of acquiring a knowledge base on well-functioning individuals and families with good social and survival skills. Because the African American family in the past has been, and continues to be, portrayed as dysfunctional, oral history can serve as a useful tool to help professional educators and students understand African American experience from the teller's point of view.

A wealth of historical data about African American survival remains unrecorded. It is important to preserve this information, not only to interpret the past for the present generation but also to provide a broader knowledge base for future generations, who then might be motivated by these historical insights to work to ensure that "racial degradation, exploitation and segregation will not be perpetuated" (Martin, 1987, p. 7).

Oral history can reveal the human diversities in the African American experience, showing how the experience is different for people within the subculture. Yet as oral histories are conducted and tapes are transcribed, the interviewer can begin to understand that "African American families, like African American individuals, are like all other families in the United States, like some other families, and like no other African American families all at the same time" (Solomon, 1976, p. 181). One also learns how coping techniques have differed. Cafferty and Chestang (1976) offer this graphic description of the African American experience:

> The African American experience connotes the deferred dreams and frus-
> trated aspirations of a people oppressed by society. It may also convey the
> ideas of a culture, style and social pattern developed to cope with life situations
> to which society consigns the African American man [or woman]. (p. 61)

The African American experience is best understood if viewed from three conditions that according to Cafferty and Chestang (1976) are

> "socially determined" and "institutionally supported": social injustice, societal
> inconsistencies and personal impotence. . . . These conditions, together with
> the development of competence in a behavioral style designed to combat
> their negative consequences, represent the progenitors of African American
> character. (p. 62)

Oral history helps to broaden the awareness of the interdependence between family, community, and political systems and of the psychological forces within the wider society that impinge on the African American family. Oral history also enhances the appreciation of these effects on the quality of family life, including the manner by which families have adapted, coped, floundered, and succeeded (Martin, 1987).

The life model framework discussed briefly in Chapter 2 was used to understand oral history. This framework was selected because it provides a transactional view that incorporates human diversity (race, ethnicity, gender, culture, sexual orientation, and physical and mental disability) as well as environmental diversity (economic, political, and social).

Germain and Gitterman (1980) present a life model of social work practice that is based on social purpose, the ecological perspective, a conceptual framework, and a practice method. The social purpose calls for a practice method that is designed to engage people's strength and the forces pushing toward growth and to influence organizational structures, other social systems, and physical settings so they will be more responsive to people's needs.

Germain and Gitterman (1980) treat stress as a psychosocial condition generated by discrepancies between needs and capacities on one hand and environmental qualities on the other. Stress, they feel, arises in three interrelated areas of living: life transactions, environmental negotiations, and interpersonal processes. A life transition might include changes that occur developmentally, as in adolescent pregnancy, and the status change from student to motherhood, from the role of good student, daughter, and sister to the role of breadwinner and caretaker. According to Germain and Gitterman, these life transitions, as well as all life transitions, require changes in self-image, in the way of looking at the world, in the processing of information derived from cognition, in perceptions and feelings, in patterns of relating to others, in the way environmental resources are used, and in the goals one has established. All require the restructuring of one's life, new adaptive behavior patterns, and new coping skills. These categories, then, reflect the achievement of competence, autonomy, relatedness and identity, and a repertoire of coping skills. They also reflect how nutrients are needed to help the adolescent mothers make the life transition to motherhood.

Unresponsive environments also can be a source of great stress. For example, when the opportunity structure is taken away or is closed to African American adolescents because of race, class, sex, and age, adaptive capacities may not be released. Organizations designed to meet adaptive needs (i.e., schools, welfare organizations, hospitals, and mental health centers) may impose stress through unresponsive policies and procedures.

Relatives, friends, or neighbors may be absent or unresponsive, may not understand the importance of goal setting, and may not have knowledge of what organizations might offer. They also may lack political savvy to challenge the system when faced with poor economical conditions, overcrowded housing, lack of job opportunities, and other hazards. On the other hand, they may be present, knowledgeable, and supportive.

In addition to life transitions and environmental unresponsiveness, stress may be experienced because of relationship patterns within the group itself. These maladaptive processes may include inconsistent expectations, exploitative relationships, and poor communication between individuals, between the new parents, between female and male adolescents, and between family members within and among the groups.

THE NARRATIVES: ORAL HISTORIES OF AFRICAN AMERICAN ADOLESCENT MOTHERS

PARTICIPANTS AND SETTING

The following narratives are the oral history stories of two teenage mothers selected from several interviews that I conducted. In presenting their oral histories, I make no effort to generalize findings because the stories reflect actual experiences and language; communicate thoughts, values, and knowledge; and are a touch of reality itself.

Unfortunately, much of the knowledge of teenage pregnancy draws from generalized research findings or practice examples. Studies describe teenage pregnancy as resulting in poverty, dropping out of school, going on welfare, and having large families (Chilman, 1983; Furstenberg, Lincoln, & Menken, 1981). There are also variables that defy these generalizations. To expand knowledge about adolescent pregnancy and motherhood, we must meet these adolescents, learn about them as the unique people they are, and listen to their unique experiences. In oral history, the adolescents tell their stories in their own words, including how they adapted. For this reason, I have not changed their manner of expression or grammar. The adolescents define and describe the nutritive environmental qualities that enabled them to survive, develop, and obtain success. Reflected in their narratives are voice tone, affect, body cues, the reality of the mother relating to her child, habits, neighborhood, and the mother's life as she lives it on a day-by-day basis.

I chose to sample mothers in their 20s looking back rather than mothers in the throes of the experience to get a time perspective, a progression of lives, and a more longitudinal outlook. The following narratives present a view of what actually happened as a result of adolescent motherhood. Using a coping, adaptation, and life model framework, I organized the facts of each woman's life in categories such as the path to adulthood and an autonomous self, including family structure, relationships and reactions, knowledge of health services and health consequences, responsibilities of motherhood, and the nutritive qualities of the environment, including available resources to support goals. Last, I present a profile of the mothers a decade later and the fruition of their lives.

A PATH TO ADULTHOOD
AND AN AUTONOMOUS SELF

The following narrative demonstrates unrealistic goal setting, inconsistent expectations, and poor communication but also shows Arnell's understanding that she disappointed her guardian. Arnell's mother gave birth to 13 children, but only 10 of them were living at the time of the interview. Most of the children were raised by a different person. Arnell's guardian was really a cousin who raised many of the kids from her relatives' large families, including her older sister and her two cousins, whom she legally adopted. She later raised Arnell's niece and nephew. Arnell said of the father:

My father did not live at home either. He lived in town, but he never really supported us. I think my father had a lot of outside children too. And it was like I was almost the baby until, like after me, there was three other kids. I was separated from those kids because I lived with my guardian, but—I think we lack the male figure in the house, someone to really talk with us. We had older sisters, but they really didn't talk with us. They always told us what not to do.

When I first became pregnant, I was trying to live for my guardian. We had never sat down to work out goals for me, but she had always told me that if I didn't get pregnant, she was going to give me this trip to New York. And then I had enrolled in this airline school, and she was telling me if I got this job, she could travel free. It was more like I was trying to fulfill her expectations rather than my own. But I think when I became pregnant I know I hurt her, and she was disappointed, but it made me feel more like it was time for me to start living for me and not other people. It was hard because I didn't have *any skills,* I didn't have *a job,* and I was still *in high school.* I was 16 going on 17, but I was in the 12th grade. But it was hard because I didn't have a job. (Arnell)

The following narratives discuss the shame, guilt, fear, and worry these adolescents experienced when they realized they were pregnant.

I was scared. I was worried. I was upset. I was wondering what she was going to think. (Arnell)

Betty is the youngest of four sisters. She first gave birth at age 16. Her father died in his 30s when she was 4 years old. Betty felt that if she had had a father living with the family, she would have had a different male image. She would have known better what type of man her boyfriend really was and could better have judged character.

I was ashamed and I felt like I let my mother down. Because she use to tell me, go to school, do something, travel, learn the world, and she always thought I wasn't into stuff like that. But I couldn't talk to her about it. I was afraid to talk to her about it. And she had no idea. It wasn't something that I planned on. (Betty)

RELATIONSHIPS AND REACTION

The following narratives discuss male-female relationships. They show the adolescents' view of their worth as women. Betty expresses the belief that the only way to attract and hold on to the young man was to have sex with him. The disappointment came when she became pregnant and he ended the relationship.

It was just something that I was more talked into by other girls. They use to tell me that if you don't have sex with this guy, how you gonna keep him? He was a very popular guy at the time at another high school. He was older than I was, and some girls told me—if you don't sleep with him he gonna get another girl. And I was so young, and I was crazy in love, that I did anything just to keep him. We only had sex three times. I didn't see him the whole time I was pregnant. Well, my cousin told him and he said it wasn't his, so I didn't bother him about it. And after I had the baby, his mother, she came to the hospital. His cousin worked there in the maternity ward and she told his mother. From day one, he never supported the baby. (Betty)

The paternal grandparents have provided emotional support as well as financial and child care resources. The example shows how supportive kin have provided important environmental supports that have fostered growth-building qualities for the child and the mother.

Like Betty, Arnell had expectations from the baby's father that did not materialize. Both she and Betty said that these young men were from middle-class families; the girls at the time had not considered that the men had goals of going to college. They also felt that the baby would somehow seal the relationship with the father. The following narratives show how wrong they were.

He never even bought her a birthday card. He thought of it as his child. He wanted her to call him father, but he never, you know, contributed as a father. To this day now, she will be 12 this Friday, and we have never sat down and talked, period, never. We never spoke 20 words between us. But he knows that his daughter, she lives there. Well, she lives with me and she be there [at his parents'] on the weekend and they, just they, been really good to her. (Betty)

Arnell describes what happened with the father of her baby when he found out she was pregnant:

When I just found out I was pregnant, my brother and his wife had sat up this master plan where they was going to give me an abortion. So, I went and told my baby's father about it and he went, "No, we make that and what does a baby need? A baby's needs are not that great and I will help you—I'll help you take care of it." My guardian always told me that when I have that baby that will be my child. I couldn't understand that, because I had always thought of it as "our child," and it was like he was there, he didn't get lost, but he really didn't do what he was supposed to do. (Arnell)

KNOWLEDGE OF HEALTH
SERVICES AND HEALTH CONSEQUENCES

In the two narratives below, these young mothers express and understand on a cognitive, as well as an affective, level the need for good prenatal-outreach health care to prevent low birth weight and infant mortality.

What was really sad was that we lived right near the health department. They had all the information there, but they never reached out to the African American community to help tell children what it was all about. They never held the classes where you could go to get this information. Most of the information we received we got from each other or when somebody else went through the health department. (Arnell)

The following narrative relates to Gibbs's (1989) research findings that African American adolescents, as compared with their White cohorts, are less well informed about contraception, less positive about its use, and less effective about using it.

When I went and got my pills, I was so naive because they did a Pap smear on me, and my mother didn't know about it. And when I didn't have my period I thought the test did something to stop my period. Because I didn't even know I was pregnant. I thought it was the Pap when they did the test. And I kept waiting and waiting, you know. I didn't tell anyone for a while because I didn't know what to do; my mother would buy the supply for the month and I would take it and throw mine away. I wish I had told her sooner. And when I had my daughter, she was underweight because I didn't go and get the vitamins and iron pills right away. I tried to hide it as long as I could. That another thing too, I think that's why a lot of babies be born underweight and are slow learning. Because we be pregnant and don't know what to do, and when we get pregnant, some of them don't know how to take care of themselves and the baby when they get pregnant. (Betty)

RESPONSIBILITIES OF MOTHERHOOD

The narrative below describes some of the difficulties these women experienced as they attempted to make the transition to the responsibilities of motherhood. Not only were some relatives unable to provide financial support but also they did not always communicate support by words and action.

Gibbs (1989) summarizes the research on Black families' communica-tion patterns to acquaint readers with ethnographic evidence that in some low-income families, parent-child communication tends to be authoritarian, critical, unidirectional, and confrontational. She states that "overt expressions of affection, nurturance, support and praise are not frequent in these families, and self-deprecative humor may be used as a protective mechanism to preserve one's self esteem" (p. 198).

> Even I was planning to go on to school. I went a half a semester at the community college. I think I would have stayed longer, if I had had someone to help me and push me, but it was so hard with the baby crying. She cried all night, and my mama used to say to me, "Well, that's your child." She bought food and whatever, but taking care of it, she didn't do that. 'Cause when I was in school, her father's mother used to take care of her. In fact, they used to keep her for a week at a time because I didn't have a way to get her back and forth. That's one of the reasons why I stopped and got a job and got my own apartment. Because for me it was hard living at home. My sisters complained about the baby when the baby cried and different things, and I just decided it was my baby, and it was time for me to go ahead. When I had my child, I had my own place. So I stopped school, got my own apartment, got a job. I moved into my own apartment when I was 17 years old. It was hard. It was no enjoyment whatsoever. It was work and home. It was hard. (Betty)

The following narrative helps readers understand this adolescent's subjective reality and a view of how she mourns her lost childhood.

> I remember that after I had her and everything like, and I used to want to go to softball games. In fact, in the apartment complex in which I live, my mother used to tell me, "Well I'm not going to watch her while you go over to the game. You got a baby, you stay here and watch her." So I couldn't even walk over to the softball games. And some of the evenings, like on Saturdays, there used to be this band and they used to get together and play. And I wanted to go over and listen to the music. And I couldn't take her out in the night air, so I was at home. I was stuck home. I missed out on a lot because of the baby. (Betty)

THE ENVIRONMENT

The following narrative appears to confirm that these women had a peer culture. It may be surmised that peer group pressure gave sanction and provided interpersonal prestige to adolescent pregnancy. One might also question whether this peer culture is a new family system for these adolescents. Can it be that the group is their substitute family and the adolescents are responding to that family and the rules of that family?

Betty also lives in the project. It was like, look what we were up against, I thought. We had one friend who was 11 when she became pregnant. Another was 12, and another was 13. So I felt like we did well from what we were up against. (Arnell)

When one got pregnant, we all got pregnant. Cause I was the first one. It was five of us who ran together. It was like one set, then the other set, then you, then me, and it just went on and on and on. And the girls from the other side of town called us the Baby Makers. We all had babies. And we found that the difference between the girls in our neighborhood and Riverhead High School, was abortions. They had babies also, but they had abortions. But we kept ours. And that was the difference.

Yes, the girls from the other side did a lot of finger pointing. They called us Baby Makers. Some of the girls were going with the same guy—one guy was going with like three girls. A lot of girls too got pregnant just because—Helen got pregnant with Mai's father just because I had a baby. She had two kids from him. Every girl got pregnant by him. He would dump them. (Betty)

GOALS VERSUS RESOURCES

The following narrative encompasses Parson's (1989) concept of "locus of internality" (p. 28). This concept deals with an individual's perception of having an impact on his or her environment. In this narrative, Arnell perceives herself as unable to influence her environment.

I think I became pregnant because I didn't have any goals set for myself. I was almost in 12th grade. First of all, I didn't think I could have a baby. It happened so easily. I felt like I wasn't going to do anything else anyway. I wasn't going to go to college. I wasn't gonna do nothing—to have a baby is nothing, so I didn't really look at it seriously. Then I think, if I probably would have sat down and set some goals for myself, maybe I would have handled things differently. You know, if you plan to go to school you can't take a baby with you. But I didn't have any desire to do anything else.

I decided that I would go to college when my little boy was 2 years old. And I was working at this hospital and I think back then I don't think they had that minimum wage law in effect, and it was almost like I was just working to take care of him. And I said to myself, this ain't going to get it. And then I decided, if I go to college at least one day I would be able to provide a better life for us. (Arnell)

These women came to realize that action plays a "crucial role in coping and adaptation. When one has an effect upon her environment, takes responsibility for an aspect of her situation, and makes decisions in areas that count, one's self-esteem is strengthened, and the skills for further mastery are developed" (Germain & Gitterman, 1980, p. 20). In the following narratives, the women's perceptions of their inabilities to influence their environment are shared. They both wanted college but perceived it as out of their control to get it even though one was offered a scholarship.

> I always wanted to go to college, but as I said, I think if I had had someone to help me and push me, we didn't really have much. My mother, she worked, but what she had went to bills. And then too we had this principal, Mr. Brooks, he got me this scholarship to college, but then I wasn't able to go away to college because I had Mai. But then I went out to Eastern—I always wanted to go to school, but then I came out a year early. You know—I wanted to go to school and make something of myself, but ended up in the same rut. I always wanted to go. I always wanted to be a nurse, but one of these days. (Betty)

Below, Arnell discusses other obstacles and describes the subjective reality of a teenage mother's world. One obstacle is the lack of a nearby 4-year college. If Arnell is to realize her dreams of a college education, she must make new life transitions of moving away from home and living alone with her child for the first time in her life. In fact, Arnell described those new transitions as fearful, saying, "I was so afraid in my apartment, I was a nervous wreck each time I heard noise or voices in the hallway. I piled chairs against the door, so afraid someone may break in."

> In my home town, they only had a 2-year college. And I knew that I wanted to obtain a B.S. Degree, and Texas was the closest. And plus my brother lived there. And I thought I would have a little support system if I moved there. But maybe I couldn't study because I was so worried about everything else going on at home. And see a lot of people don't look at that—they don't look at what's going on at home. They just look at your grades. They don't know what it took to get there, or what it took to come to school every day. Too, like with a lot of the teenagers, they don't know the struggle those children had. (Arnell)

A DECADE LATER: THE FRUITION OF LIVES

With much perseverance, Arnell has earned her B.S.W. and is currently working in an alternative school program for teenage mothers. She often begins her work with a client by stating, "I'm one of you. . . . It's our problem." She is able to use and share her life experiences helpfully. She is married. Her son, Kareem, is now 9 and has a positive relationship with her husband, his stepfather. They are homeowners and upwardly mobile.

Her son is an affectionate child, is doing well in school, and is active in sports. Arnell feels the family as a whole needs to spend more time together, to play games together, to communicate openly about sexual development and household management, and to feel loved. Kareem's father is well employed but does not contribute to Kareem's financial or emotional support.

Betty is a health aide at a cancer research center. She finished high school and still hopes someday to pursue nurses' training because she loves her work. She has learned so much through her job. Working with young women with cervical cancer, AIDS, and other illnesses has had a sobering influence on her in one sense and has stirred up anger in another. The sobering effect is a result of the human waste; the anger is because no one helped the patients learn about the misuse of their bodies when they were younger. At 28, she is a single mother of three children, ages 11, 8, and 2½. She worries that she expects too much of her daughter, Mai. Because Mai is a physically mature child, Betty fears she may depend on Mai too much and expect her to assume adult responsibility. "Some days, when we be tired, we make them grow up too fast. . . . They have to grow up a lot faster than they are able to handle things, because I am at work and they are home alone." Betty also experienced fear that Mai's physical development may force her into an early sexual relationship, for which neither she nor Mai is prepared. Mai's father is now married and does not contribute to Mai's financial or emotional support, but his parents are still active in Mai's life.

ANALYSIS AND CONCLUSIONS

The two women presented in this chapter seem to challenge some of the stereotypes about teenage mothers. Although they each experienced a period of time on Aid to Families With Dependent Children (AFDC), both are now fully employed at satisfying jobs. Despite many obstacles, each completed high school, and Arnell graduated from college as well. They do not have large families. Both have developed a sense of positive self-esteem and have a sense of competence as individuals and as parents with demonstrated insights into family life and pressures.

The women were able to make the positive changes in their lives through their own adaptive abilities and coping skills. This process covered the life span and supportive qualities of the environment, including parents, relatives, peers, and organizational systems.

Gibbs (1989) discusses the development of self-esteem by drawing on Spencer's (1982) findings that self-concept in Black children and adolescents is shaped by responses they receive from relations and peers of their same race. Drawing further on Rosenberg's theses (1979), Gibbs (1989) concludes that "an assessment of Black adolescent self-esteem must take into account the adolescent's subjective evaluation of assets and liabilities" (p. 193). Arnell and Betty, as presented in this chapter, describe their assets as two high school diplomas and one college degree, decent jobs, a caring husband, the ability to buy a new home, and happy children. Liabilities are still the struggles for full financial security and the obstacles faced as they seek to realize further career aspirations.

Despite the initial disappointments experienced by each woman's mother or guardian on learning of the pregnancy, families did pull together eventually and offer support. This was particularly evident when the women began to develop clear goals for education and vocation. This shift seemed to happen for each young woman as she experienced her autonomy and felt enough power within to realize her goals. One might say that the locus of internality deepened with greater maturity and successful life experience. This, of course, could be tested with empirical research. But the matter of resources to obtain goals, particularly for Betty, the single parent, continued to be troublesome.

The relationship with the child's father remained the most unresolved and in some ways the most problematic area. Clearly in these two situations, the teenage fathers did not assume responsibility, and this affected the lives of the women and their children profoundly. Preventive work with young Black men appears to be necessary to reduce the incidence of teenage pregnancy and to enhance the roles of fathers in Black family life.

The young women showed remarkable resilience and coping abilities under difficult circumstances. Their values and insights on family life are remarkably astute and moving. From these two lives, everyone can learn a great deal. We learn the reality of their worlds and that people grow beyond generalized predictions and expectations. We learn that family, financial, educational, and environmental resources are needed for this growth. Oral history has helped demonstrate the strengths of each life and has been an effective tool in the reaffirmation of the capabilities of people.

REFERENCES

Billingsley, A. (1987). Black families in a changing society. In J. Dewart (Ed.), *The state of Black America* (pp. 99-103). New York: National Urban League.

Cafferty, P. S. J., & Chestang, L. (1976). *The diverse society: Implications for social policy.* Washington, DC: National Association of Social Work.

Chilman, C. (1983). *Adolescent sexuality in a changing American society.* New York: John Wiley.

Furstenberg, F., Jr., Lincoln, R., & Menken, J. (1981). *Teenage sexuality, pregnancy and childbearing.* Philadelphia: University of Pennsylvania Press.

Germain, C. B. (Ed.). (1979). *Social work practice, people and environment: An ecological perspective.* New York: Columbia University Press.

Germain, C. B., & Gitterman, A. (1980). *The life model of social work practice.* New York: Columbia University Press.

Gibbs, J. T. (1989). Black American adolescents. In J. T. Gibbs, L. H. Huang, & Associates (Eds.), *Children of color: Psychological interventions with minority youth* (pp. 179-223). San Francisco: Jossey-Bass.

Martin, R. R. (1987). Oral history in social work education: Chronicling the Black experience. *Journal of Social Work Education, 23*(3), 5-10.

Martin, R. R. (1988). Black family adaptation, survival and growth strategies: An oral history research project. In A. Rodgers (Ed.), *Black family at the crossroads of development* (pp. 80-113). Columbia: University of South Carolina, College of Social Work.

Martin, R. R. (1991). Oral history methodology: Examination of issues among adolescent mothers. *Family Science Review, 4*(3), 109-122.

Moynihan, D. (1965). The Negro family: The case for national action: A transaction social science and public police report. In L. Rainwater & W. L. Yance (Eds.), *The Moynihan report and the politics of controversy* (pp. 39-125). Cambridge: MIT Press.

Parson, R. J. (1989). Empowerment for the role alternatives for low income minority girls. In J. A. B. Lee (Ed.), *Group work with the poor and oppressed* (pp. 27-45). New York: Hayworth.

Rosenberg, M. (1979). *Conceiving the self.* New York: Basic Books.

Solomon, B. B. (1976). *Black empowerment: Social work in oppressed communities.* New York: Columbia University Press.

Spencer, M. B. (1982). Personal and group identity of Black children: An alternative synthesis. *Genetic Psychology Monographs, 106,* 59-84.

10

UNDERSTANDING COMMUNITIES
The Pliny Street Block Association

SELECTION OF THE TOPIC

This chapter presents oral history as a means of understanding African American and other minority communities. The research described here was an oral history project about a community-organized block association on Pliny Street in Hartford, Connecticut. Graduate social work students taking my oral history course conducted oral histories with members of the Pliny Street Block Association, located in a working and low-income urban African American community with some middle-class residents. The community, in recent history, had been mainly a comfortable working- and middle-class Jewish neighborhood with residents whose occupations were professional and business owners. Today, this neighborhood is troubled by current urban issues such as the drug epidemic, crime, AIDS, unemployment, and school problems.

DEFINING THE SELECTED ISSUES

First, the research students developed broader knowledge and understanding of the community, including the community's history and the

AUTHOR'S NOTE: This chapter includes narrative extracts from interviews and data collected as part of a research project conducted January through May 1991 by students in my oral history course in the School of Social Work at the University of Connecticut, West Hartford.

founding of the block association. They learned the city planning committee's definitions of community needs and objectives and how well the city was meeting these needs. These definitions were not always congruent with the block association members' perceptions of the problems and their effect on the community.

Second, rather than understanding the community solely on the basis of "problems," students learned to identify community strengths. These include community networking, social supports, leadership and programs for youth, housing, and so forth. In addition, students discovered that a relatively large number of African American families own their own multifamily homes and are landlords and that this particular community has remained one of the most stable African American communities in this city.

Third, this approach allowed students to restore human traits to research participants depersonalized by other methods and reinforced student understanding of the necessity for building rapport with African American clients. Fourth, oral history interviews with community residents and community leaders helped develop networking skills and contacts for graduate students. Last, the finished product (the oral history itself) became archival material and served as a contribution to the community in its continuing efforts at self-affirmation.

HISTORICAL OVERVIEW

Pliny Street, named for the son of a settler, is part of the Clay Hill-Arsenal neighborhood, located just north of downtown Hartford and centering on Main Street and Albany Avenue. The neighborhood was named for the clay soil found there and a former state arsenal, which had been demolished.

Clay-Arsenal is one of Hartford's oldest neighborhoods. Its development began in the late 1800s, by which time multifamily housing was predominant. The area was home to the Irish and other working people at the time. It served as a port of entry for immigrants into the area.

As early as 1860, the African American population established themselves in this area, centering on Talcott Street Church, a Black Congregational church. Connecticut Valley tobacco growers began recruiting large numbers of southern African Americans during the World War I era. This resulted in the large population growth of African Americans in Hartford's north end. The only areas open to those populations during World War I were Clay Hill and South Arsenal. The minority population continued to grow in this area through the 1960s as Puerto Ricans were recruited to work in the tobacco fields.

The Clay-Arsenal area went through tremendous deterioration and disinvestment, which resulted in the area becoming one of the poorest in the city. Riots and civil disturbances in the 1960s forced many retailers to go out of business. Many residents fled the area and changes in the population's characteristics began. The population declined by nearly 3,600 residents between 1960 and 1970 and by about 6,400 between 1970 and 1980.

DESCRIPTION OF
PARTICIPANTS AND SETTING

Twenty-eight members of the Pliny Street Block Association were asked to participate in this project. Seventeen individuals (5 men, 12 women) agreed to be interviewed, ranging in age from early 30s to early 80s. The interviews were conducted using the oral history research methodology. The interviewees are referred to in this research project as narrators. All the narrators signed consent forms, which described the purpose of the project and requested their participation.

Eight research questions were designed. Each of the individuals interviewed was asked these questions or variations of these questions during their interviews. Spontaneous questions were also asked. The research questions were as follows:

1. What is the demographic information about the narrator?
2. What is the history of Pliny Street?
3. How did the Pliny Street Block Association begin?
4. What are the purpose and goals of the association?
5. How does the Pliny Street Block Association affect the community?
6. How satisfied are the members with the Pliny Street Block Association?
7. What are the current projects of the block association? What are the past projects?
8. How does the block association serve and/or affect different generational groups in the community (i.e., children and youth)?

DATA ANALYSIS

The research students took total responsibility for conducting the interviews and transcribing them into narrative format; they also did some of the data analysis. I read the narratives for individual and collective themes and organized them into categories designed to tell a comprehensive story of the narrators' views. The categories illustrated in the following narratives are (a) the beginning of the association, (b) life on Pliny Street, (c) activities of the block association, (d) youth, and (e) empowerment/the group's strengths and weaknesses. The raw, unedited narratives can be used by future researchers to search for new meanings and to interpret the narratives from several perspectives.

BEGINNINGS OF
THE BLOCK ASSOCIATION

The president of the Pliny Street Block Association describes the history of the origins of the association:

In 1978, in February, I cannot recall the exact date, there was a tragic fire on Pliny Street. It was then, 45-47 Pliny. There was a young woman and her two small children that perished in the fire because vehicles were parked blocking the street. We had a terrific snowstorm . . . a terrific amount of snow and the combination of the cars trying to come in and out, and people not obeying the snow ban and not being able to get out. And then the street was completely closed and as a result of that the fire apparatus could not get around.

It was a really very tragic thing because what appeared for the next week was (if you can picture this in your mind's eye) the shell of the building. The structure did not fall down but was all charred . . . and the next morning all the icicles were shining with the rising sun. Like, you know, a symbol. And they removed the building. They allowed the neighbors and the media to come in. There was a whole lot of flurry and that was not the kind of thing we are used to on Pliny Street.

They [neighborhood leaders] went to some of the old community leaders. They were active in the 1960s and said, "We used to have a group up there called the Pliny Street Improvement Association," which was made up of residents of Pliny Street in the 60s.

They came by my house. It was in March of 1979. I thought, I'm going to participate because what happened in that tragic fire is something that I never want to forget about, and I would like to work with my neighbors to see that it doesn't happen again. That was my personal interest at that time. And while I committed myself to involvement, they did not come to Pliny Street because of the fire, they came because it just so happened that the timing fell that way. But for me, it was heartfelt. My grandmother lives on the street and she knew the woman who had perished. There were still old folks there. They did not have the smoke detector law yet.

We had a street-sweeping operation there that involved two trucks. We said we're gonna have a cleanup! We had everybody notified. They had flyers on the car, on the vehicles. We had bullhorns out there, rakes and shovels, city crew. Later we got the city workfare crew.

We've involved the Boy Scouts, and the Cub Scouts in later years. Since they formed this chapter [Boy Scout], we now support it. The cleanup has been an annual event, which has not been held the last few years only because now there aren't too many vacant lots. We're at a different level now, if that's private land, we make the property owner people clean it up.

We got publicity both positively and adversely. Sometimes you need a little of that too, to make people click. Because you know, you upset somebody, they'll come to your meeting real quick. You can beg and present films in front of their face and they won't come, but as soon as you tow their car because they sit out there for 3 weeks, when they're only supposed to sit out there 3 hours.

LIFE ON PLINY STREET

Two longtime residents describe what it was like in the area.

I had a store right on the corner [as she points in the direction of its location]. Right there, on that corner over there: Brooks and Mather. I worked to do housework. From that I got the store and I was there for 20 years. Well, things got so bad I had to give it up. You know, breaking in and robbing. . . . I was held up many times but I never got hurt. I guess they figured I was an old lady and they just never shoot me or hit me. So, I just figured it was a little too much for me and I got out of there. (80-year-old woman)

I think our greatest strength is in our caring and sharing for each other. We truly care about each other and we share with each other and I think that is our greatest strength right there because whatever happens to one of us, happens to all of us. And the other thing is, many of the people who live on the street have lived here for a number of years. I think it was at one time, like, 95% ownership, but now it's down to maybe about 50-50.

At one time there were a lot of professional people that lived on the street. We had schoolteachers, there were five ministers on this street at one time; firefighters, including myself, police officers, detectives. The gentleman I bought this house from was a member of the 99th Pursuit Squadron during World War II. He was a fighter pilot. Maybe you heard of the famed Black Pursuit Squadron that fought in Europe during World War II? His name was Aaron Gastins, he was the one I bought this house from. (Longtime male resident)

ACTIVITIES OF THE BLOCK ASSOCIATION

The president describes the various activities of the association:

We don't send out the kind of stuff that we used to send out in the old days, with the kinda faded type and so forth. I mean we try to be professional and I'm trying to get a new letterhead with our new emblem, membership cards, and maybe a membership discount from local merchants for members.

And I've got a listing of all the property owners, so that we can send a letter to each and every one. I've got the software that I could be able to do this. But I haven't had the time. But I mean this is the thing we need: more members because the idea is support us in unity, if not in person.

In the earlier days of our organization, the term member was loosely defined. So that if you come in, it was a dollar a month. We talked about making it $12 a year. But then they said no, people cannot afford that! So for 3 years we kept it like, when you put a dollar in, you are a member for this month. But you see, when you start offering membership benefits . . . like when somebody or an immediate member of your family goes into the hospital, we send a $10 get-well gift (the Cheer Fund). Now you gotta define membership, you see, because you're using the members' money to give. So we evolved from the lackadaisical kind of loosely defined member into a nicely defined member. But still, it could be further defined because people want that identification. I mean, they want that sense of belonging. "Here's your membership card. This is what we want you to do this year."

Last Christmas we delivered fruit baskets to the sick and shut-in on our block. I'm the Cub Master of the neighborhood Cub Scouts that the association financed. The Cub Scouts distributed the fruit baskets to the sick and shut-ins. As far as I know, the association would deal with anything and everything to better the block.

Another thing we got done is the streets needed to be resurfaced, and we got new sidewalks and curbstones put in, just by being together as a group. There was one period when, through the Community Renewal Team, we got paint to paint houses.

At one time we were patrolling the street to make sure people weren't getting broken into and getting their pocketbooks snatched on the street, and breaking into cars and things of that sort. Kids sometimes, you know, come around and vandalize your property and all those kind of things.

At one point we did have two-way communications. They would have a walkie-talkie and someone would be in a house or place, manning a base station. If there was a fire or a criminal act of some kind, they would radio to them and they would then call the authorities. We were very successful with that and the level of success was maintained for quite a long time.

YOUTH

Three narrators discuss young people:

I oversee the children and I encourage the children to do planning on their own. They do allow children into their plan when there's something like an annual day like the Pliny Street Block Association Day. We need more facilities for these kids. Good facilities so we don't have to really worry about people taking advantage of them. And it has to be somebody that knows what they are doing. I give piano lessons. I tutor. Two of the kids on my street were runoffs in a spelling bee. So next year, we're going to be winners. You know, we're going to say, "Pliny Street has the best spellers." That's what I tell the kids. And I try to always push them into being things. We have some kids on the bottom, but try to push them to do. I have about 16 Explorers, and the ones that are of age every Friday they do volunteer work at the Hartford Hospital. They've been doing it for 3 years. As soon as they get old enough they go into training. Pretty soon now we are going to have the largest volunteer staff at Hartford Hospital. (Retired schoolteacher)

The involvement with the youth was a slow development because it seems that the average age group of our membership seemed to be higher. So the outlook on the youth was indignation. Where were they in the cleanup? Where did they come out? We haven't seen anything. Why don't they pick up? You know, they'd see a few of the disrespectful ones, whenever there'd be a commotion. There wasn't a real rapport. We had sponsored a Back to School Family Day. We spent approximately 50% of our treasury. We closed the street off, we had dancing, and barbecue, and a horseback riding, and pony rides, and disco dancing. (President, Pliny Street Block Association)

For the 40 years I've lived here, it has changed a lot. You never used to see kids out past 9:00. When the street light comes on, they knew it was time to come in. And it was the same with most people up and down the street who had kids. (Male member in his 70s)

WHY THEY HAVE ENDURED:
STRENGTHS, WEAKNESSES, AND EMPOWERMENT

I'd like to add that the Pliny Street Block Association is an inspiration to me 'cause I see a positive in this great negative community of ours. Cocaine, crack, has torn a great hole in the north end of Hartford with young minds. And I see no change. In North Hartford, there's a church on every street. I noticed that a lot of these church members don't live in North Hartford. They're raised Baptist, for example, but it's [the church] not in Bloomfield, or Manchester, or Rocky Hill; they commute in and they commute back out.

And they don't realize their church has a neighborhood too. I had a vision that I share with people today: If these people in church would get out those 2½ to 3 hours that they have morning service on Sunday, and just grab their Bibles and walk around their local neighborhood of the church, singing a song or praying or just walking around, maybe it will make some difference. (Male member in his 30s)

When I got my siding, the neighbor down the street liked the way my home looked so she got hers done. Then, the man across the street, he had his done. Then his friend, and it kept on. So all the way down the street, the people wanted to get their houses sided. So just about all the homes on the street have been improved within the last 10 years, except just one down there that I know. One person do something, then they like the way it looks, then they want to do theirs too. (Longtime female resident)

If something comes up, we deal with it. Our members bring it up and in the old days they used to say, "You people." I says, "Wait a minute right there, not 'You people,' 'us.' You wanna bring it up, you come to the meeting and you bring it up. You bring it up 'cause that's you and you are the other half of 'we.' Because I am not paid for what I do. I'm just like you, I'm your neighbor." (Male member in his 70s)

ANALYSIS

The common identification of the block parties as a visible activity suggests that block parties are centrally important to the feeling of community among the Pliny Street residents. The block watch project that the residents also frequently mentioned demonstrates a concern for neighborhood safety of people and property. It may also indicate a concern about the responsiveness of the public safety providers such as police and fire personnel. It is interesting that a tragic event catalyzed interest in the association's formation.

Narrators frequently stated that helping people was another general aim of the Pliny Street Block Association. This indicates that the group is one that places some premium on mutual aid and on having an active organization responsive to needs of neighborhood residents.

The last items that were mentioned by both men and women as activities consistent with the intentions of the association were the youth development projects. Many people expressed interest in the cultivation of options for the betterment of the children in the neighborhood. The cleanup day and the Cheer Fund were mentioned by the female respondents in their interviews. This may suggest a greater regard for the importance of these activities by the female residents of the area.

When research participants were asked what they would like to change about the block association, three major responses were given: to increase the membership, to get the youth more involved, and to "make" people more active. Fourteen participants (eight women and six men) felt that to get the youth more involved was a change they would like to see in the Pliny Street Block Association. Five men and two women indicated that increasing the membership was the change they wanted in the association. One man wanted to "make people" active.

The most common response to this question was the desire to get the youth more involved in the block association. This could be interpreted to mean that the members of the block association viewed youth as a rich resource and as the future of the community and, therefore, efforts should be made to train, preserve, and support the efforts of youth who might thereby transmit the knowledge and culture of the race and of the community. Only 7 of the 17 participants believed that the association was reaching youth.

STRENGTHS OF THE BLOCK ASSOCIATION

The narrators who participated in this oral history research project were asked what they felt were the strengths of the block association. Participants surprisingly gave the same answers. Most of the participants said that the major strength was that it gave them political clout in the area's local politics. The next most frequent answer was that the block association was a source of reference for people in the neighborhood. It kept them abreast of what was going on in their neighborhood as well as surrounding neighborhoods. The last strength mentioned was that the people of Pliny Street have really invested in the organization.

CONCLUSIONS

The narrators of these stories and the listeners became richer and empowered by the encounter because it was the first time students learned how to carry out all phases of a research project. As a class, they developed a research topic, defined its purpose, learned the oral history methodology, interviewed participants, and transcribed and analyzed data. They were also able to describe their own weaknesses in the area of interviewing, listening, and tuning in to the participants' sense of time, space, and subjective views. Students also learned that receiving a list from an organization does not always mean that each person in that organization will participate in the research.

Students were able to remove some of their myths about an African American neighborhood and developed, I hope, a level of respect for the individual and collective strengths of African American families. It was also an empowering of the neighborhood because the project documented both accomplishments and hope for the future. As a result of this written report, the association members can clearly see some of the areas they need to strengthen.

CONCLUDING REMARKS
Incorporating Oral History
in Social Work Research

As a research tool, oral history provides data that can enable learners and practitioners to rethink critical issues. This book has demonstrated the ways in which oral history is useful in helping social work educators and others gain new knowledge about African Americans and other oppressed groups who have been left out of the system. I have shown how social workers' interviewing skills can be used and enhanced in the oral history process. Several chapters have exemplified the uses of oral history in preserving and recapturing the strengths of individuals, families, groups, communities, and organizations. The ability to do oral history research adds to the constructionist perspective taking hold in social work today. This narrative approach gives life to the stories of people whose voices have been silenced for a variety of reasons.

Although no claim is made for oral history as an exclusive data-collecting method, I have found that using oral history methods can (a) restore human traits to research participants depersonalized by other sociological and psychological methods, (b) generate information from groups who are not always represented or who may have been maligned, and (c) fill gaps in the historical literature. Like any other data-gathering method, oral histories can provide baseline data from which to formulate new questions and to explore new areas of research. Oral histories provide an opportunity to learn about another culture in its historical context and to facilitate understanding of the need of building rapport with clients.

There are many ways to make oral history projects come alive to more effectively disseminate knowledge. For example, I have made slides to supplement my narratives as I shared them with professional and general audiences. I have also made videotapes of hallmark events, including church services, in the life of a researched community. This was especially moving in a project I carried out with descendants of escaped slaves in Canada.

I use this material to teach the method of interviewing and the meaning of participant observation, to show pictures of the gatekeepers, and to describe some of the difficulties and pressures sometimes experienced when conducting an interview with a number of people in the room. This material also provides researchers an opportunity to recognize repeated themes and to better understand the subjective reality of the individual and the collective meaning of the community. Researchers can also learn how to communicate across cultures and social class. Through this material, I show that yes, they too can conduct an oral history project.

In addition to using oral history material in teaching, I also publish excerpts from my oral history projects in journals and monographs and have appeared on a television show to discuss oral history when one of my oral history students, who served her internship in a news studio, refined her skills in the media. And I present to the community a copy of the finished product. It is extremely important to follow through in sharing with the participants and allowing them to become empowered.

In this book, I have also presented examples to show how oral history can be used in macropractice. I believe that readers of this book can be suited for the job, provided they are willing to invest energies in the accumulation of the necessary knowledge.

I argued throughout the book that oral history is an important tool for educators, practitioners, and ordinary people to intervene in the life of a person or of a community. In addition, I hold that sometimes a person's life is so far-reaching that it opens a "window of the world" and by so doing, makes it possible to generalize events but seldom meanings. Oral history makes the meaning of events clear to the listener.

The in-depth interviewing technique of oral history described in this book has much value for the profession of social work. It allows a level of research necessary for probably the only means by which social work researchers, practitioners, students, and other historians in the mainstream can view other cultures up close and at the same time gain the knowledge and skills that will allow them to empower and heal.

There are "many ways of knowing" (Hartman, 1990, p. 3). I invite readers to experience this art and science through the use of oral history and trust that readers will find this book a useful guide on the journey as an oral history researcher.

REFERENCE

Hartman, A. (1990). Many ways of knowing. *Journal of the National Association of Social Workers, 35*(1), 3-4.

INDEX

145

ABOUT THE AUTHOR

Ruth R. Martin, MSW, PhD, is Associate Professor and Associate Dean for Academic Affairs at the University of Connecticut, School of Social Work, in West Hartford. She received her bachelor's degree in secondary education from Tuskegee Institute and her master's degree in social work and her doctorate in professional higher education administration from the University of Connecticut. She has also taught practice at the University of South Florida at Tampa. Her extensive practice background in social welfare includes work in family agencies, psychiatric and correction institutions, and public schools. In her research and teaching, she demonstrates the goodness of fit between casework practice and oral history research.

Her chapters on oral history are included in *Black Family at the Crossroads of Development* (1988), *The State of Black Hartford, Connecticut* (1993), and *Qualitative Research in Social Work* (1994). Her articles have appeared in publications, including the *Journal of Social Work Education* and *Family Science Review.* She has often presented papers at professional conferences on the use of oral history in social work education.